GREAT COMFORT

GREAT COMFORT

G. Kaye

MACMILLAN

Great Comfort

© Geraldine Kaye 1988

© Illustration and design Macmillan Boleswa Publishers (Pty) Ltd 1997

All rights reserved. No part of this publication may be reproduced, stored in a retrieval system, or transmitted in any form or by any means, electronic, photocopying, recording, or otherwise, without the prior written permission of the copyright holder or in accordance with the provisions of the Copyright Act, 1912 (as amended).
Any person who does any unauthorised act in relation to this publication may be liable for criminal prosecution and civil claims for damages.

First published in 1988 by
André Deutsch Limited
105-106 Great Russell Street, London WC1B 3LJ

The South African edition published 1997 by
Macmillan Boleswa Publishers (Pty) Ltd
P O Box 1235, Manzini, Swaziland

Typeset in New Baskerville 11/12.5
Cover design by Jennifer Henning
Cover illustrations by Alan Kennedy and David Huggins

ISBN 0 7978 1051 X

Printed by Sigma Press

Great Comfort

Comfort has lived in England with her grandmother since the death of her English mother, but goes to Ghana to stay with her father for the summer. Though he greets her with delight and warmth, she soon senses that all is not well. Her stepmother has returned to her own village to have a baby, taking Comfort's little stepbrother with her. Comfort goes to visit her Ghanaian grandmother in the family village, longing to be accepted; but her terms are too hard for them. How can you belong if you only stay for a week or two?

Comfort's problem is how to make other people understand. She is herself – not a white child in Ghana because of her English mother, nor a black child in England because of her Ghanaian father, but simply Comfort Kwatey-Jones who must make her own decisions.

Acknowledgements

I wish to acknowledge my debt to the numerous people who have studied and written about Ghana and in particular to Margaret Field for her book 'Social Organisation of the Ga', my former husband, Barrington Kaye, for his book 'Bringing up Children in Ghana', Deborah Dellow for 'Women in Accra', 1977, and Christine Oppong for 'Middle Class Marriage', 1977.

In a country where people originate from tribal groups with different languages and customs and where, in addition, some people are westernised in outlook whilst others live much as their forefathers have lived for centuries, it is difficult to identify a common culture. Ghanaians are often an enigma to each other. A writer has an obligation to strive for accuracy but has to be ultimately free to make an imaginative leap – without which fiction does not live.

Finally I wish to thank all the Ghanaian people I met in the four years I lived and worked there for their exceptional friendliness and good-humour, which made my time in Ghana, in some ways, the most memorable years of my life.

Chapter 1

The letter was lying on the hall table. A square of blue island in a shining mahogany sea. Had it been there that morning, Comfort wondered as she picked it up. Had she missed it. That was impossible surely. It must have come by the second post.

The silence of half-term had already descended on the boarding house of Lodge School after the frenetic activity of Speech Day and her feet on the stairs made a sad, hollow sound. People came and people went, sometimes they went for ever, Comfort thought. As Margaret had gone for ever, and Ruby, not that she had really liked Ruby.

In the dormitory she sat on the bed beside her suitcase, staring at the letter in her hand with its flowery pink Ghanaian stamp, extending the moment of anticipation. Letters and parcels were always better before you opened them. It was natural law.

Her diary lay on the top of the suitcase and extending the moment further, Comfort flicked to June 14th and wrote, *Yesterday was Speech Day.*

Strawberry teas. All the parents came but Granny and Grandad didn't. Granny doesn't like speechifying. Comfort sighed and licked the pencil and wrote very black. *Letter from Mante.* She called him Mante to herself because Margaret had called him Mante but when they were together he was Father of course. Sometimes she wondered about Dad but it was difficult to say Dad to somebody you hadn't seen for a very long time and hardly knew. Besides Mante talked of respect for elders and ungrateful children being like ashes in the mouth of parents and she wasn't sure he would care for the familiarity of Dad.

Suppose she didn't open the letter at all, Comfort wondered, how long would it keep its savour. She knew what was in it, guessed at least, guessing made her heart beat faster.

"Aren't you going home then?" Suzanne demanded, breathless, clattering up the stairs and scooping her case and blazer off her bed.

"My granny and grandad are coming to fetch me, Granny and Grandad Barton," Comfort said embarrassed, smiling and half-expecting Suzanne to ask, "Are they the English ones?"

At Lodge School they asked things politely, obliquely with a sideways glance. The kids at school in London would have said, "Black or white?" But Suzanne was busy with her own concerns, away and clattering down again before Comfort had even finished.

Footsteps on the front path.

A blue car waiting. "Hello, darling." Doors slamming and the car drawing away.

After that it was quiet again. Suzanne gone, Maxine gone, everyone gone home. Dust floating in the sunlight. Downstairs the hall clock ticked which you only noticed at night in the ordinary way.

Where was her home exactly, Comfort wondered. Home was where you kept your hairbrush, Maxine said, spinning back and forth between England and Hong Kong. Home was where you kept your photos, Suzanne said. At this moment home was in her suitcase either way, Comfort thought. She relied on Maxine and Suzanne to tell her what everyone else at Lodge School seemed to know by instinct. Once she had fitted in at schools all over London with no trouble at all. Once she had known how, home had been where Margaret was.

She jumped up suddenly and peeled the School Aid poster of Bob Geldof from the wall over her bed. "Half-term" she murmured, massaging the blue-tac between her fingers and packing that too. His eyes screwed up against the African sun, must get sick of staring across the dormitory at Suzanne's poster of James Dean and Maxine's of Duran Duran day after day. Home was where Bob Geldof was. The whole world was home for Bob Geldof.

Comfort slid her thumb into the envelope. It was time for the letter. Letter-time.

When a taxi drew into the kerb five minutes later Comfort was fizzing inside like a catherine wheel. She had guessed right, Mante wanted her in Ghana for the summer holidays. But it might be better not to mention the letter for a bit because Granny wasn't going to like it. When would be the best time. In the train or after supper or tomorrow perhaps, because Granny got so fussed travelling all the way to Folkestone and back.

Down in the hall Granny was talking to Miss Beale in the special bell-voice she used for such occasions.

"Oh, there you are, Comfort, dear," Miss Beale said and her voice was special too, her talking-to-parents voice but extra cheery because it was half-term and her toe nails were varnished rosy-pink in her summer sandals. Miss Beale had a boyfriend, Suzanne said, anyone could tell. "All ready for the off then, are we, Little Miss Forgetful? You'll forget your head one of these days, Comfort," she added with a trill of silvery laughter.

"Oh, sorry," Comfort said smiling. She smiled and said sorry a lot.

"The taxi's waiting, dear," Granny said flustered, pecking abstractedly at Comfort's cheek. Behind her Grandad smiled and nodded, resigned to the hustle and bustle of travelling but hating it.

"Come along then, do, you two slow-coaches, we'll just get the 3.55 if we're lucky," Granny said, shepherding them towards the taxi with her arms spread. "How are you, dear?" she added a few moments later as they drove towards the station. "How was Speech Day? Can't stand all that speechifying myself, never could. Some people just like the sound of their own voice."

"You really don't *need* to come and fetch me," Comfort said frowning. "I am fourteen and if you told Miss Beale it was okay I could just get the train by myself."

"What did she mean, 'Little Miss Forgetful'"? Granny's eyes were bright as blue glass and curious.

"Dunno," Comfort shrugged, though she knew right enough. It was a warning. Miss Beale had moods. On one of her off days she went through the boarding house like a dose of salts. Notices, *Please switch off the lights* and *Please leave the bath as you would like to find it* went up along the corridor and "No talking up there" shouted through the bannisters after lights out. Had a row with her boyfriend, Suzanne said, pre-menstrual tension, Maxine said. But hadn't it all got worse since Ruby went, Comfort wondered.

"You young girls always want to run before you can walk," Granny said. "I daresay I was just the same. But I couldn't let you travel on your own, dear, I'd never forgive myself ... never ... if anything happened ... all the dreadful things one reads in the papers. Besides your Grandad wouldn't hear of it, would you?"

"Makes a nice day out for us, Comfort," Grandad offered, conciliatory, as the taxi turned into the station yard. "Good bracing air, Folkestone. Always liked the place." As he got out he fumbled apprehensively for his wallet, always elusive at moments like this.

"What did he charge you, then?" Granny said, peonypink and brisk as they stepped towards the platform where the train was already waiting. "Daylight robbery. They see you coming, always did."

"The thing is I could get the bus by myself and it would be much cheaper," Comfort persisted though she knew it would make no difference. Getting angry might make a difference but awful things happened when people got angry. "If only you'd let me ..."

"Be a nice state of affairs if we couldn't be bothered to fetch you, dear," Granny said as they settled into the carriage. "You are our own granddaughter after all."

It was something she said quite often, as if she had to remind herself, as if she had never quite got over the shock of a black grandchild, or so it seemed to Comfort. She considered the letter in the pocket of her blazer, her fingers making sure it was still there. It seemed deceitful not to mention it.

"Our only granddaughter," Grandad murmured glancing away out of the window where orchards slid past, long lines of trees with small green apples the size of marbles. "Margaret's little girl."

"Not so little," Granny said brightly, trying to dismiss the thought that had grabbed all three of them at the same instant. Such sadness, such grief, but where was the sense in brooding? "You'll be out of that blazer in no time at all. You should have had the bigger size. I said so in the shop."

"It's three years tomorrow," Comfort said in a low voice. June 15th. How could she have so nearly forgotten? She heard again the crash like a hundred dustbin lids all dropped at once and the long long silence which followed. At first she had dreamed about it night after night. But not any more. Now she knew right through her being what at first she had refused to accept, that Margaret had been killed that morning in Kensington three years ago. That Margaret, her mother, was dead.

Penfold in Kent, the village where Granny and Grandad had lived since Grandad retired, had changed dramatically in the six weeks since Comfort had left after the Easter holidays. Long midsummer grass dotted with buttercups covered the green, swishing as you walked, and the two beech trees, planted to commemorate V.E. Day and still bare when she went back, were all rich copper leaves. The forget-me-nots and wall-flowers which had lined the front path of Smithy Cottage had faded and the rose bush, Grandad's favourite Albertine, had hundreds of salmon pink buds which paled almost cream as they came out, filling the garden with their fragrance.

"Home at last, thank goodness," Granny said, fretted by the journey. "And now there's the meal to get."

"Can I do something?" Comfort said. Was Smithy Cottage home she wondered, one of her homes.

"That poinsettia you gave us at Christmas-time has done us proud," Grandad said nodding towards leaves still splashed with crimson. "A real bobby dazzler."

"No, no, dear, I left everything ready," Granny said. "It won't take me a moment to heat the soup. Take your case straight upstairs, we don't want your bits and pieces all round the sitting-room, do we?"

"Okay," said Comfort. "Oh, sorry, Granny." Okay was her favourite word since she had discovered it came from an African word *okeah*. But it was not Granny's favourite word.

Grandad had retreated to the sanctuary of the garden shed and the placid companionship of his pipe and seedlings. The stairs curled round in the thick wall of the cottage as in a double-decker bus and Comfort stomped up and round and then up again to the attic bedroom tucked under the roof. The bedroom was shaped like a ridge tent with the ceiling sloping down either side, even in the middle it was only just above Comfort's head. Dormer windows looked out at the back and front. Everything seemed so small, doll's house size after school.

Half-term and freedom, no more getting-up buzzer and lights-out buzzer and two-p. fines if you forgot your gym shoes. Comfort bounced on the bed twice and then slithered out of her green gingham dress and dark green blazer, like a snake shedding its skin. Margaret's ring, which she wore on a string round her neck and never took off, fell against her chin as she scufffled in the chest of drawers for jeans and scarlet tee-shirt. The tee-shirt was too tight and she ballooned out the front with her hands. She had come out a lot since last summer as well as coming on. And if her body was changing on the outside, she was changing inside too, thoughts and feelings.

The trouble was she didn't know what she wanted any more, didn't know how she felt even, because one minute she was all right and the next she was furious. Nobody had ever been as furious. In the old days with Margaret, she had said and done more or less what she liked, what came naturally. But now she had to do what Granny liked and Lodge School wanted and nobody ever asked her what she wanted. Sometimes Comfort wanted to scream and shout like the day before yesterday when Miss Beale suddenly came into the bathroom. "Comfort Kwatey-Jones, you know perfectly well it's not your bathnight, so may I ask why you're washing your hair?" But, because of Ruby, Comfort didn't scream or shout, she just smiled and said, "Sorry, Miss Beale, I forgot. Sorry."

Ruby was something different. There were not many black girls at Lodge School, two older girls from Malawi who went everywhere together, and three West Indian girls in Comfort's class, Ruby, Joleen and Charlene. Council sent her, paid her fees and all, Ruby said with some complacency, had this special meeting, didn't they, wasn't nobody else could handle her terrible tempers, wasn't no other way.

"What are you doing, Ruby Watts?" Miss Beale had said in one of her moods. "What's it look like, Miss?" Ruby said, cheeky. "But you know perfectly well that you only wash your hair when it's your bathnight," Miss Beale said. "Piss off," Ruby said. "I wash *my* hair when *I* want." "I shall have to phone your social worker," Miss Beale said thin lipped and suddenly Ruby went wild. The bathroom stool flew though the window and landed on the pavement with a tinkle of glass. Later that evening Ruby went. A special school, somebody said, but nobody knew for certain, except she would never come back. It was a month since Ruby went. Awful things happened when people got angry, Comfort had always known that and Ruby was proof.

The discarded green uniform reproached her from the floor and she pushed it into the drawer and slammed it shut. She deposited her brush and comb in the dressing-table, making Smithy Cottage her home and stuck Bob Geldof high above the bed so he could see out of the window, right across the green to the little stone church, wreathed round with yew and chestnut trees, and the flat vista of the Romney Marshes beyond. Too much water, he'd like that surely, a nice change after Africa. Refreshing.

The photos, snaps taken in the patio garden of Hillside Estate in Ghana, went nicely round the edge of the dressing-table mirror. Mante in dazzling white shirt and trousers, smiled expansively, Efua, her stepmother, with her airhostess cap tipped jauntily, smiled her professional smile of welcome, little Jeo Peter held out

Lambkin, the toy Comfort had sent for his second birthday.

Jeo would be bigger by now, almost three, her only brother; no wonder she wanted to see him so much. A child got its body from its mother and its spirit from its father, Mante said, so she and Jeo had the same spirit. Did they look alike? Comfort peered at the snap. Her skin was lighter, of course, because her mother, Margaret, had been white, but the eyes were the same, surely, large round eyes like black grapes. And yet not the same. There was something strange and sad about Jeo's eyes, and for all hers were dark and her mother's had been blue, Comfort's eyes were like Margaret's, lively eyes alight with humour.

Tomato soup mingled with the scent of Albertine and drew her to the window. Miles of flat green land and then the sea and more skyline than anywhere else, it seemed. Below Granny emerged from the front door and tinkled the bell for Comfort. She had bought the bell, a cow-bell, on holiday in Switzerland. A moment later she tinkled the bell from the back door for Grandad in the shed, completing a familiar ritual.

"That was quick work, my dear," Grandad said, rubbing his hands appreciatively. "We're hungry as hunters, eh, Comfort?"

"It was all left ready," Granny said, gratified by the compliment and her own efficiency, as she handed bowls of steaming soup through the hatch. Ham and salad and a loaf of brown bread were already on the table. "I always leave everything ready when I know I'm going to be tired. But I haven't done any *croutons*." Granny shut the hatch and came round to the dining room. "It's no good you two wanting *croutons* when I've been all the way to Folkestone and back at my time of life," she asserted as if they had protested. "You'll have to do without *croutons* tonight."

"Better without them," Grandad said.

"I could travel perfectly well on my own," Comfort murmured; the second time that day and at least the tenth time in the past two years. "I mean some girls are fetched by car but …"

"I don't think you quite understand, dear," Granny said, carefully tilting her soup spoon. "You are getting to be … well a big girl … and young girls … well you can't trust anybody these days."

"I can," said Comfort.

"There's no necessity to be cheeky, dear," Granny said.

"Sorry," said Comfort.

"Don't catch us giving up our day by the sea, Comfort," Grandad said with a wink. "Only chance we get."

"There's plenty of places nearer for the sea," Granny said tartly. "Put your napkin in your collar, Barty, do. I've quite enough to do without cleaning tomato soup off your best tie all tomorrow."

"Anyway …" Comfort said and her voice sounded odd and breathless. She hated it when people got cross, awful things happened when people got cross and said unforgivable words. And what she hated most was Granny getting cross at Grandad who never snapped back.

"Anyway …" she repeated because what was the good of waiting for the right moment when there never would be a right moment. "Anyway I've had a letter."

"Letter?" Granny echoed. She put down her

11

soup spoon, almost dropped it. The colour drained from her face as if she knew what was in the letter already. How could she know.

"And I've got to get used to travelling on my own because my father wants me to go to Ghana for the summer holidays, and he's written to the school and he's sending the ticket in a fortnight, so it's all arranged."

"Arranged?" Granny dabbed at her lips with her napkin, and then wiped two drops where the soup had spattered on the polished table. There was a long moment of silence. "Nobody's said anything to me. After all that upset last summer … everything cancelled at the last minute … the disappointment … "

"But he couldn't help it … I mean Efua was ill in hospital. People can't help getting ill and cancelling things, can they? Besides, Grandad sent me on that canoeing holiday instead, so I wasn't all that disappointed in the end," Comfort said, talking fast. She didn't like it when Granny talked about Mante, you could tell she didn't like him, never had. "It was magic that canoeing holiday."

But she had been disappointed, crying all night, with her face stuffed into the pillow, because of Granny and Grandad asleep just below, and the wide gaps in the old oak floorboards. A *tragedy*, that marriage, Granny had said, Comfort had heard her quite distinctly. Nothing but trouble from start to finish.

"Well, you won't get another canoeing holiday if you're disappointed again, young lady, so don't think it," Granny said, getting up suddenly and gathering the plates together. A bright pink patch had appeared on either cheek now. "Your grandad's not made of money."

"Oh, I know ..." Comfort said, trying to think of the right words. It was awful upsetting Granny who always did her best and wrote every week and taught her how to make spaghetti bolognaise and apple crumble and bought her clothes and sewed on name-tapes. Granny who cared so much about everything, like her school reports and getting good marks, and wanted Comfort to stay at Smithy Cottage every holiday. "But the thing is ... the thing is ... Efua's having a baby in August and they want me to go out there ... and, well, the baby is my little brother or sister ... and then there's my other grandmother in Wanwangeri, she wants to see me, too, and like you always say, 'Grandmothers have rights too', so that's that, isn't it?" Comfort smiled with a simplicity she did not feel, knowing that was far from being that. Hadn't Grandmother in Wanwangeri wanted her to stay for ever?

"Course you must go," Grandad said gruffly. "Be with your father ... your own people ... family ... your little brother."

"And what are *we*, may I ask?" Granny asked, posting a square inch of ham into the small slot of her mouth.

"You're my family, too," Comfort said quickly. "My English family." A child belonged to its family, Mante said, but if you had two families in different countries, Comfort wondered, where did you *really* belong then.

"Let-downs and disappointments all over again, that's what it'll be," Granny said and there was the glint of tears in her eyes now. "Don't say I didn't warn you. Have you waiting on her hand and foot she will, your stepmother, like some poor little servant girl ... I know her sort ... but nobody cares what I think ... nobody."

"Now, my dear," Grandad said. "It's only a couple of months ... surely we can spare our Comfort for one summer holiday."

"Go then, go," Granny said and her voice quavered ominously.

"I'll write every week, really I will," Comfort said. She hated it when people got upset, awful things happened, but what could she do? "Okay, Granny? Oh, sorry ... sorry."

Outside the garden gate creaked and Lettie Stamp came up the garden path, smiling broadly, heavy footed and wearing a blue dress that reached below her knees, plenty of room for next year's growth.

"Trust that one to be round before we've had time to draw breath," Granny scolded.

"I'll get it," Comfort said, jumping up with relief as the front door bell rang.

Chapter 2

"You got here, then," Lettie said grinning and putting her arm through Comfort's and leading her across the village green, their legs swishing in the grass. "It's ever so nice to see you. Seems like ages ago since the Easter holidays."

"Seems like yonks," Comfort agreed smiling shyly and glancing sideways. She was pleased to see Lettie and even more pleased that Lettie, the only girl in the village her age, was pleased to see her. But you had to be careful what you said with Lettie, who went up the wall at the least thing and you never knew beforehand what. First she'd give you a mouthful and then she'd sulk for days. You had to be different careful with different people, Comfort thought, it was a different kind of careful with Maxine and what was all right with Granny in Penfold certainly wasn't all right with Grandmother in Wanwangeri. Since the letter from Mante she had begun to think a lot about Grandmother in Wanwangeri.

"Don't think your granny likes me," Lettie said, pouting and wanting a contradiction.

"Don't think she likes me much," Comfort said surprising herself and crossing her fingers because it was a mean thing to say. But she wondered if it was true all the same.

"You're rotten you are." Lettie was shocked. "'Course she likes you. She's *got* to like you whether she wants to or not because you're her granddaughter. She's got to *love* you."

"Mm," Comfort murmured, non-committally. Fetching her from Folkestone and wanting her to be top of the class was a kind of loving, she supposed. Wanting you to stay for ever was a kind of loving. Anyway, people couldn't help how they felt, so it wasn't fair to blame them.

They crossed the lane in the warm evening light, yellow as apricots, and Comfort glanced towards the school. Her arrival three years ago had been a great event in Penfold, rivetting imaginations. Nobody had ever seen a black girl before except on the telly and the village children's eyes, blue as sea and grey as water, stared and stared. Comfort was used to that. In London they stared and wrote things on walls as well like, "Keep Britain white" and "Blacks go home", but where was home when Comfort had been born in London. In Penfold when she first came, every child in the school had painted her, pictures of a black face had been pinned all round the schoolroom, kids' pictures, but the pictures had gone in the dustbin long since and everyone was used to Comfort now she had spent every holiday and half-term in the village for two years.

"Evening … er … Comfort, back from school, is it?" Mr Watkins said friendly, nodding in her direction on his way to the Woolpack Inn, a long low building standing on a slight rise opposite the church.

"Lovely little old evening ... er ... Comfort," Mr Jarret said going in the same direction. His feet crunched on the gravel drive and his eyes lingered on Comfort's tight red tee-shirt and fixed there like glue, his lips were wet.

"Got your eyeful?" Lettie shouted bridling, bursting into explosive giggles as he tripped at the door. "You want to watch where you're going, you do, Frank Jarrett."

Comfort crossed her arms, holding her elbows and smiling but hating the intrusive stare of Mr Jarrett's glittering eyes. At boarding school you didn't get things like that, never got used to it, didn't have the chance.

In Wanwangeri, men like Mr Jarrett, restless, middle-aged men, took a young girl as second wife. Not that Comfort fancied being anybody's second wife. No thank you. No way.

"Dirty old man," Lettie's face was scarlet. "Just let him stare at me like that, he wouldn't dare. Let's go round the churchyard, be more private.

"Will it be all right?" Comfort said uncertainly as they moved into the shadow of the high chestnut trees which bordered the churchyard. "I mean the rector told us ..."

"Who's he think he is?" Lettie said, pausing at the lychgate and glaring down the lane towards the Rectory. "I'm in the choir aren't I and I've lived here all my life and my grannies and great-grannies for hundreds of years, so I got more right round the churchyard than rector who's a blinking foreigner only been here seven flipping years."

"Mm," said Comfort wondering why Lettie got so

steamed up about everything. Would she have been more angry if Frank Jarrett had stared at her? Or less.

The church stood on a higher rise, a ridge which bordered the village separating it from the stretch of marshes beyond. Lettie perched herself on the marble edge of her grandmother's grave proprietorially; *Letitia Stamp*, engraved and painted in gold. She patted the space beside her, inviting Comfort to sit down. The marble was fish-cold but the stone wall of the old church behind them gave off the stored warmth of the summer day, its rough grey surface patterned with lichen, rust, ochre and pale sea-green. Beyond was an orchard where sheep grazed under sparse, gnarled apple trees and then the flat expanse of the Romney Marshes, squares of green and earth brown criss-crossed with the straight lines of the banks and rhynes which kept them drained. And beyond was the distant sea, a grey line luminous and shining as silver.

"What's new in the village, then?" Comfort said after a pause. She didn't want to talk about the letter, not yet, not with Lettie all worked up. Lettie was bound to resent the letter, Comfort going out to Africa. Nowadays Lettie resented everything.

"Not a lot," said Lettie with a discontented sigh. "Nothing ever happens in this dump." Her thick dark eyebrows drew together above her large eyes, green as gooseberries. "Mrs Watkins got another baby and our Alan got married and there's council houses going up on the glebe field." She counted on her fingers. "How about you? Still friends with that Chinese girl?"

"Maxine?" Comfort said diffidently. Her other friends, school friends, was another delicate subject best avoided.

"Yeah, Maxine. Flown to Hong-Kong for her half-term, has she? Course they're all stinking rich, Chinese." Lettie spread the skirt of her dress over her knees, the bright metallic blue shone in the sun like a shiny seaside postcard.

"She's staying with an uncle who's got a restaurant in Soho," Comfort said.

"Can't stand chinky food myself," Lettie said with a sniff. "What's it called, her uncle's place?"

"New World, I think," Comfort said.

"It's a new world all right, all those Pakis and foreigners and that coming here like they do."

"Anyway Maxine's only half-Chinese, her mother's Eurasian," Comfort said. It sounded like an apology.

"Oh-ah," said Lettie. "What's that when it's at home? My dad says it's not right all those people coming from Hong Kong and everywhere and filling up our schools and taking our jobs." She turned her head and looked at Comfort. "Do you think it's right?"

"Depends," Comfort said, conciliatory. She was used to these second-hand skirmishes with Lettie's father, used to parrying. It was the way she had to be in England, the way she was. Anyway there was no point in arguing with Lettie who jumped like a grasshopper this way and that, so you never got anywhere except cross. Besides if she once got into a sulk, it would last all half-term and spoil everything. You couldn't win with Lettie.

"Blinking cheek I call it," she said, pulling a bit of long grass and biting the end reflectively. "Them filling up our posh boarding schools, so all we English kids got left is your state schools, your rundown comprehensives."

"But my boarding school is a state school ... Lodge School is meant especially for girls whose parents are overseas and that," Comfort explained not for the first time. "I mean you needn't think it's posh or anything ..."

"Yeah, well, it's our blinking taxes pays for it then, that's what my dad says any road." Lettie shifted restlessly. "Know any boys?"

"Boys?" Comfort echoed. "Not really."

"Do you think you'll marry a black boy or a white boy?" Lettie said ruminatively.

"Dunno, do I," Comfort shrugged and smiled, but she found the question irksome. Once it had been all right to be black, Margaret had loved and married Mante after all. But black wasn't a sufficient reason for liking somebody, and at Lodge School she resented the general expectation that she should be friends with other black girls like Ruby and Joleen and Charlene. At first, after missing a year at school, Comfort had been bottom of the form but she was fifth at the end of the first year and second now. Maxine was top, Maxine was bright and worked hard too. If Comfort couldn't like girls just because they were black, how could she like boys just for that reason? Winston Silcott was black for instance.

"Course you don't know, but you must think about it, surely?" Lettie said. That was true of course. Comfort couldn't help thinking about it any more than she could help thinking about the yellow-haired choir boy who had smiled in her direction during the sermon. He had hovered in her thoughts like a brimstone butterfly ever since. Somebody said his name was Martin. Bob Geldof lived in her head too. Before that it had been

Kwame, son of Sika, headman in Wanwangeri. They had climbed a mango tree together, Comfort and Kwame, and sat side by side in the fragile privacy of leaves. It was a long time ago, she was eleven then.

"I suppose it all depends who wants to marry *you?*" Lettie said. Comfort said nothing, looking down at her legs and tracing a path on her brown calf with one finger just as Kwame's finger had traced. They hadn't kissed. In Wanwangeri people didn't kiss.

"I mean …" Lettie went on with a quick sideways glance. "I mean not everybody would want to marry a black girl, would they? Our Alan wouldn't, that I do know. Chocolate drops, we call them at our school. Don't suppose there's any boy in this village would want to marry a chocolate drop."

"Suits me," Comfort muttered in a strangled voice. Lettie was being mean on purpose, spiteful. People behaved like that because they were frightened or unhappy, Margaret said. Comfort was angry but it didn't do to show anger. Suppose she was to scream and shout and throw things like Ruby. Awful things happened when people got angry like in Brixton that night, years ago, screams and fires and glass tinkling on the pavement. It was cutting your nose to spite her face. Now Ruby was gone. Lost.

"Not meaning anything … but … you got to think of the kids, haven't you? Have you heard that rhyme … the woman who had quads … one black and one white and two khaki," Lettie went into peals of laughter, Comfort smiled wanly. Chocolate drop, toffee, nougat and peppermint, she thought.

"You shouldn't talk like that."

"Why ever not?" Lettie said innocently. "It's a free country, isn't it?"

"Because it's ignorant," Comfort muttered.

"Who you calling ignorant?" Lettie said, bridling. "The blinking cheek of it. Anyway ... There's something I got to ask you ... " she glanced conspiratorially over her shoulder. There was nothing but grass and tombstones, ancient granite, white Victorian marble and modern synthetic composition. Her eyes, green and round, seemed to grow slightly protuberant. "Have you done it yet?" Comfort shook her head.

"No? Well I suppose you haven't had the chance with no boys at your school," Lettie said pityingly and then changing tack after a pause she added. "Me neither, matter of fact. Well, my mum'd kill me, wouldn't she? Know what she does, looks in my drawer every month. Well there's all blinking boys at our school, can't stand them myself, and all the teachers got their knives into me and my dad gives me stick all the flipping time because of the wicked lies in my school reports." Lettie sighed gustily. "Don't catch me stopping on once I'm sixteen. Do my own thing."

Swallows swooped back and forth across the churchyard, catching insects on the wing and the chestnut trees cast lengthening dark shadows. Swallows went to Africa too, would they have gone before she got back, Comfort wondered. Penfold was all right now she knew everybody and who was whose cousin. But a village wasn't just the now people, it was the people who had gone before, people who had made the fields and cottages, people who came and went. Romans had drained the marshes, Grandad said. They had gone away leaving it drained. They had also left the brown eyes which cropped up here and there in the predominantly blue and grey. Didn't Lettie's little brother, Bob, have brown eyes? Lettie's family probably had Roman blood but they might not like to think so.

"What are you going to do if you do leave school?" Comfort asked.

"How should I know?" Lettie shrugged her shoulders violently as if to throw off a heavy load. "Get a job working in a shop, wouldn't mind. Or a hairdresser, wouldn't mind. Probably end up on the dole. Well you do if you're 'C' stream don't you, especially with all these foreigners taking all the decent jobs. Anyway, what are you going to do?"

"Don't know yet," Comfort said shifting a little and feeling the ring against her skin and hearing Margaret's words, "You'll make brain surgeon, shouldn't wonder, Comfort Jones." Brain surgeon was a joke, of course. Or was it? Comfort was good at Physics and Maths and Granny wanted her to be clever and two girls from the sixth form of Lodge School had gone off to study medicine last year. But it wouldn't do to say anything like that to Lettie. She had to pretend to be stupid with Lettie. Suzanne said it was clever to pretend to be stupid with boys. But Maxine said girls with good salaries got plenty of boys.

"Better not sit here for too long, getting piles," Lettie said, though she didn't get up. "Course you've got brains, that's your trouble. Probably go for a teacher."

"No way," Comfort said.

"Bet you will," Lettie said gazing across the marshes, chin in hand. The sunset reflected in her wide eyes looked like little pink flames. "Your lot are taking all the decent jobs and leaving all the hard graft for us. That's your new world for you."

"Shops and hairdressing aren't that hard graft." Comfort suggested, taking a risk. Lettie could so easily stomp off.

"Nothings hard graft when you don't have to do it," Lettie said truculently, "that's what my dad says any road."

"My dad's asked me to go out to Ghana for the summer holidays," Comfort said tiring of the quagmire of Lettie's dismal moods. She hadn't meant to say it until right at the end of half-term.

"Rather you than me," Lettie said with an exaggerated shudder. "Don't catch me going places where there's all them snakes and scorpions. And suppose they don't let you come back?"

"Course they will," Comfort said. "I got to go back to school, haven't I?"

"One for the pot." Lettie exploded into a paroxysm of laughter. "Get it? Can't argue with a hungry man if you're his dinner, can you? One for the pot."

"Stupid," Comfort said.

"Who are you calling stupid?" Lettie demanded, sticking out her lower lip aggressively but then collapsing into helpless giggles again. "Cannibals, aren't they, some of them, and they're all starving in Africa, we had about that at school, about Bob what's-his-name. One for the pot … One for the pot." Lettie used both hands to straighten her face down into solemn lines. "Sorry."

"In Ghana there was an ancient civilisation … an empire … when everybody here was all in woad …" Comfort said. "My dad's writing a book about it."

"Is that right?" Lettie said, standing up and stretching her arms. "Well good luck to him. When are you going back to school?"

"Wednesday," Comfort said.

"Ooh, posh," Lettie said in a tone which hovered between triumph and resentment. "We got the whole week off our school. I'll be picking strawberries. You make a bomb picking strawberries. Want to come?"

"Don't mind," said Comfort.

"Haven't upset you, have I?"

It was almost dark when Comfort got back. Bats zigzagged in the dusk and the chestnut trees were black against the waning peach of the distant sky and squares of yellow light showed in cottage windows round the green.

"What time do you call this then?" Granny said, looking over the top of her spectacles. Both she and Grandad were reading, nursing mugs of hot milk. "You ought to be in bed long since, girl your age."

"Sorry," Comfort said.

"It is her half-term holiday," Grandad murmured.

"Never mind half-term, it's far too late for a girl her age to be out on her own."

"I wasn't on my own," Comfort said. "I was with Lettie."

"That girl," Granny rolled her eyes towards the beamed cottage ceiling expressively. "That Lettie Stamp. I've heated up your Ovaltine twice already."

"Sorry," Comfort said, but why did she have to say sorry all the time when inside she was still fuming. "Why are you always going on at me?"

"I beg your pardon?" Granny's shoulders were suddenly stiff.

"I said I wish you'd stop going on at me," Comfort

said in a louder voice.

"What sort of thing is that to say to your grandmother?" Granny's cheeks had flushed pink.

"Well … well you get sick of people going on at you," Comfort said lamely and her voice quavered because it wasn't fair getting cross with Granny just because she didn't dare get cross with Lettie. Just because she knew Granny would never desert her however cross she got.

In the kitchen she poured milk into the waiting mug and clattered the saucepan into the sink. Half-term, she thought, half-term was no buzzer for getting up and no buzzer for lights out but it wasn't doing what you wanted.

"Better make the most of the child while she is here …" Grandad's gruff whisper came through the hatch.

"Spoiling," Granny snorted. "Just like you spoilt our Margaret, and look where it got you. No kindness in the long run … spoiling a girl like Comfort."

In the attic bedroom Comfort sat up in bed with her diary. June 15th, *I hate Lettie. How dare she. I hate her, I hate her, I hate her. And I hate Granny too.* She wrote in small black letters pressing hard. A diary was meant for the truth. But it wasn't true. Well it was a bit true sometimes. But just writing it seemed to change the truth, melted the anger away, Comfort stared at the words a moment and then began to fill them in, making them into small grey bricks. Margaret had never hated anybody. People couldn't help being like they were, Margaret said, which was all very well.

Comfort bit the end of her pencil and considered the space left. It was quite dark outside now, the window a square of black, a moth fluttered at the lampshade, beating its wings. She looked at the photographs for inspiration: the white dazzle of Mante's shirt, Jeo and his woolly lamb, Efua smiling in her Ghana Airways cap, Bob Geldof in the poster above, unshaven and in the shadow he might almost be a black man. In her head he was singing *This is the World Calling*. What did she want, Comfort wondered.

Going to Africa she wrote, that was what she wanted. *Going to see Mante*, that was what she wanted too, and that was who she loved. *And Jeo*, to see Jeo was what she wanted more than anything, to see her little brother who was almost three. That was natural, wasn't it? If a person's spirit came from their father, she and Jeo had the same spirit.

Chapter 3

Comfort worked her way steadily down the banked-up lines of strawberries which ran the length of the large sloping field, her hands darting into neat green leaves with serrated edges like fish teeth. Most of the strawberries went into the large basket but now and then she popped one into her mouth, pressing it hard with her tongue until it exploded into sweet-sour juiciness. Pawpaw had something of the same sweet-sour juiciness, she thought. But in Wanwangeri the soil was laterite or "swish", rusty-red rather than brown, and cassava and yam were planted in clumps not straight lines.

At eleven Comfort had spent a whole year in Ghana, partly with her father but mostly living in her grandmother's village. She had learnt how to live, learnt all that was expected of a girl her age by the Ga people, her father's tribe and her own. She had made her own farm, grown yams and cassava for food, and worked at her grandmother's cloth stall in the Akwapawa market too.

The market had been brilliant. If she went to

Ghana she would have to go to Wanwangeri to see Grandmother and to the market at Akwapawa too. Comfort smiled to herself, remembering. She had been cloth-clever, business-clever like her grandmother, everyone said so, and in Ghana it was all right to be pleased when people gave you admiration and compliments, not like Lodge School where modest self-depreciation was the approved response.

But it was more than that. Comfort had found herself in the market, discovering skills she didn't know she had, making up new and even more persuasive calls every day and the market women had listened. The way they laughed and clapped at her jokes had pleased and excited her as nothing else ever had. Actors on stage must feel like this, Comfort thought, famous people like Terry Wogan, stars. She had grown while she was in Ghana, not just in inches. The heart of Ghanaian people was formidable, Mante said, warmer and more generous than all other hearts. Ever since, Comfort felt as if a little bit had broken off and lodged inside her own heart, she was half-Ghanaian after all.

But Comfort had come back to England though Grandmother had wanted her to stay and nobody argued with Grandmother. Did that mean that she could never go back to Wanwangeri? Comfort had had to put her Ghanaian life away from her as if she were closing a book. She had to go to an English boarding school and catch up on the year she had missed. There were new rules to be learnt now, rules people would tell you like always standing up when the teacher came in the classroom and more subtle rules you had to find out for yourself like it not-being-done to sit next to prefects at meals unless you were asked. And as well as Lodge School, Granny had lots of not-done rules.

"Nice one, Comfort, you're a good quick picker," Mr Davis said, weighing her basket and marking his book.

"Thanks," said Comfort, her thoughts summoned back to Penfold in Kent. The back of the Range Rover was already piled with strawberry punnets. Mr Davis in shirt sleeves, arms reddened by the sun, was the most important man in the village, owner of much land and provider of casual employment. But you couldn't say he was headman exactly, Comfort thought. He smiled too much for one thing and the rector was better for advice and understanding all the forms and allowances, and besides the only ceremonies in Penfold were for christenings, weddings and funerals which only occurred occasionally. In Wanwangeri there were ceremonies and festivals every few days.

"One of the best pickers we've got," Mr Davis was saying. "But you're going off at midday? Back to school, is it?"

"Yes," said Comfort smiling shyly. "Sorry." In England she was always shy, saying sorry and excuse me. It was expected of a girl like her, Comfort saw it in people's eyes. Mante wasn't shy and when she had lived in Ghana she hadn't been shy either. Selling cloth from Grandmother's stall she had run all over the market calling out, "Buy my fine-fine cloth, lady." "Aye-aye, you look gay as a pineapple, lady," It was another reason for going to Ghana. She wanted to see Mante of course, and little Jeo and Grandmother and Ata and all her brothers and sisters but more than that she wanted to find the girl she had been three years ago, the "been-to" cloth-clever girl who had run and shouted in the market.

Today was Wednesday and Comfort had been picking strawberries with Lettie under the wide blue dome of sky all half-term. Her skin felt quite sore from the sun. A dozen people were working there, humped over the lines, women and older children. She and Lettie had started at the top of the field together that morning but Lettie was easily distracted. "Can't stand that wimp, Wayne Todd, don't let him see me," she had whispered loudly an hour before, running forward and missing out several well-laden plants, ostensibly so that Comfort hid her from Wayne's line of vision. But five minutes later she had made sure that Wayne did see her and now the two of them were absorbed in swapping friendly badinage.

"Fancy me rotten, that's your trouble, Lettie Stamp."

"Wouldn't fancy you if we was stuck ten years on a desert island."

Lettie wasn't shy, Comfort thought, she didn't know how to be. Was it something to do with living where your grannies and great-grannies and all your family had lived for generations. Was it something to do with living in England and being white.

Strawberry picking for Mr Davis was better than being at Smithy Cottage and Comfort needed the money. In Ghana even quite small children were expected to bring something home, and besides while her hands were busy and earning, her mind was free to think, work her way back, remember. There was Ga, for instance, the language of her people; during the year she had spent in Africa she had spoken little else. Then she had been fluent but now the words came slowly to her mind like brown leaves stirred from the bottom of a muddy pond. Kwame would have left school by now and be working in his father's pottery. What would she say when she saw Kwame? Where would she look?

Wayne and Lettie, working on rows on either side of her now were coming up the field in silence. Running out of repartee, they had thrown strawberries instead and Mr Davis, suddenly stern, had threatened to send them off. Now Lettie, crimson-stained from a direct hit, was sullen behind the thick curtain-fall of light brown hair which concealed her face.

And what about her own farm, Comfort thought. It was about half the size of a tennis court, she had cleared the bush herself and planted yam and cassava and pawpaw seeds. Probably the pawpaw trees would be tall as a house by now. Having your own farm was magic, nobody at Lodge School and no fourteen-year-old girl in Penfold had a farm of her own. Was it still hers after all this time, the ground itself belonged to Onyame, of course. Grandmother had poured libations into the rust-coloured earth turning it red as blood, asking Onyame's permission for her granddaughter, Comfort, to break the earth with her chungkol. Could she ever forgive Comfort for running away?

Another letter had arrived from Mante on Monday, addressed to Mr and Mrs Barton. Comfort had picked it up and seeing *Mante Kwatey-Jones, 3, Hillside Estate* on the back had taken her breath away. It was a polite letter about the projected visit, gracious and a bit flowery, Comfort thought privately, but didn't Mante say that respect must always be shown to older people no matter what and Granny had been somewhat mollified. That there was no mention of Jeo was a disappointment but letters were a bit like chocolates, Comfort thought, the promise on the outside, vanilla truffle or raspberry surprise, never quite fulfilled in the white or pink cream.

"This is your last supper, then," Granny had said the evening before, putting the hot meal through the hatch and coming round. "And we've hardly seen you, dear. No time to show you shepherd's pie or anything else."

"Aunt Esi taught me to make *abomu*," Comfort said suddenly. Could she still make *abomu* and *garri* and *fufu*, even the words were unfamiliar. "In Wanwangeri nobody works on Tuesday, and nobody goes fishing because it's the birthday of the river and the sea."

"That's as maybe," Granny said after a pause.

"Every Tuesday off, eh?" Grandad murmured. "Good idea that."

"All half-term strawberry picking dawn to dusk, I really don't see the necessity," Granny said fitting the lid on the dish of spring greens.

"But I like it," Comfort said.

"It'll be all round the village we don't give you enough pocket money," Granny said, spooning out shepherd's pie. "Fifteen pounds a term her grandad gives her, fifteen pounds, I told Mrs Brown in the shop."

"Is fifteen pounds enough?" Grandad inquired. "She's a great letter-writer, our Comfort, all these stamps for overseas cost money."

"Course it's enough, she twists you round her little finger," Granny said. "I told Mrs Brown this morning our Comfort twists her grandad round her little finger."

"I don't, do I, Grandad?" Comfort mumbled. "Anyway, it isn't the stamps, it's the presents."

"What presents may I ask?" Granny said. "You've no call to be giving presents, a girl your age, its ridiculous."

"Presents for Ghana. I mean, when I went before I didn't take any presents and ... I mean, well, they expected it ..." Comfort tried to explain. "Because everybody gives presents all the time in Ghana."

"Cupboard love," Granny said with a sniff. "Nobody gives me presents."

"Your lovely poinsettia?" Grandad said raising his eyebrows.

"Christmas is different," Granny said.

"It's the custom of the country, presents all the time, Mante says presents and dashes make the wheels of life go round ..." Comfort said.

"Sounds like bribery and corruption to me," Granny said. "I daresay there's a lot of Ghanaians wish they were back in the British Empire. Gold Coast it was called then."

"Oh, I don't think they do. I mean I've got to give presents ... anyway I want to ... Like I made this white woolly lamb for Jeo in handicraft last summer term ... Lambkin it's called ... all furry and soft with brown silk eyes. Miss Beale cut it out and I sewed it and stuffed it and sent it off and Jeo absolutely loves it. He's got it in the photograph Mante sent, I'll show you," Comfort said, excitedly pushing back her chair and running upstairs before Granny could stop her.

Up and down in the middle of supper was definitely not done and a bit over the top really,

Comfort thought as she ran. Was she trying out her bubbly and assertive Ghanaian self instead of her always-saying-sorry English self? Or was it something else? Jeo was her brother, her only real brother so far and thinking about him made her feel all warm and good inside. She had felt like that all the time she was making Lambkin and she would have made another lamb straight away, just to keep the feeling, but all the fur fabric was gone.

"Here it is," she held the photo out for them to see.

"Looks a jolly little chap, does Jeo," Grandad said, flicking his glasses and peering at the photograph. "And that's a very fine lamb, Comfort, a real bobby dazzler, that Lambkin."

"No good me looking when I haven't got my glasses," Granny said. "White like that, I only hope it's washable."

"Course I'd like to take him Paddington Bear when I go this time," Comfort said. "A proper one from a shop."

"A lot of silly nonsense," Granny said. "And I don't suppose it's appreciated ... a child like that. Paddington Bear indeed."

"But I like giving presents," Comfort said. She thought of her grandmother's compound in Wanwangeri. All those children who were her brothers and sisters according to their way of thinking, twelve of them, and probably several more by now. Perhaps if she took some packets of felt pens she could give them a pen or two each.

"Set your heart on going then, have you?" Granny said. "Do better to stay here and catch up with your school work. You missed a whole year's schooling, going out before, as I shall tell your father ..."

"Our Comfort was second in the form last term. Sounds to me as if she's caught up already," Grandad said. He smiled encouragingly, the eye further from Granny winked under the prawn whiskers of his eyebrows.

"62% for her Geography exam and 55% for Latin doesn't sound too brilliant to me," Granny said. She had studied Comfort's last school report and committed its details to memory. "She may seem to have caught up on the surface but still not have a proper grounding underneath. Schooling is very important for a girl, especially a girl like Comfort," Granny finished, going out to fetch the raspberry trifle from the fridge; Comfort's favourite pudding, made specially.

Later that night Comfort sat up in bed. *Strawberry picking all day*, she wrote large right across the days and then working backwards - Tuesday 18th June *Shepherd's pie and spring greens and raspberry trifle.* Monday 17th *Cold lamb and salad.* Sunday 16th. *Roast lamb, mint sauce, new potatoes, peas and apple pie and custard.* What else was there to put? Wet red lips lurked unbidden in her head and kept coming back but she wasn't going to put Frank Jarrett in her diary. No way. *Soon I shall see Kwame.*

"Are you ready, Comfort, all packed up?" Granny said, exhilarated by her smart new trouser suit and the impending journey. "Taxi'll be here in a minute. That Frank Jarrett's always late. This rate we'll miss the train."

"Frank Jarrett?" Comfort tweaked her blazer round her.

"There he is," Grandad said, standing at the window and keeping out of the way. The more fussed Granny got, the quieter he became. "He's just turning the car into the lane."

"Off we go then," Granny said. "Whatever do you look like Comfort? Your uniform all crumpled as if it's been on the floor all weekend. When I was your age I took a pride in myself, I put clothes on hangers properly and didn't go round like a ragamuffin."

"Sorry," said Comfort.

"Frank Jarrett's waiting, dear," Grandad said.

"Did you look in all your drawers and in the cupboards too?" Granny said as the front door slammed behind them. "I don't want to be sending off parcels you've forgotten for the rest of the week."

"You really don't have to come all the way to Folkestone," Comfort said as they got into the taxi. She had avoided looking in Frank Jarrett's direction as she got into the taxi, but her voice sounded breathless and a bit odd, quavery, as if she was sort of excited.

"Goodness gracious, what's all this straw in the back?" Granny was saying.

"Sorry, Missus, been shifting bales over Stone Farm all morning," Frank Jarrett said laconically.

"You could just put me on the train and let the taxi bring you straight back," Comfort said desperately. Bobby stood on the green, knee deep in grass, watching her departure, but what about Lettie. Was she still sulking in the strawberry field?

"When I was your age I didn't argue with my grandmother all the time," Granny said settling her back into the taxi. "You must learn to accept things gracefully, dear. Besides we've hardly seen you, have we, no time to show you shepherd's pie or discuss your G.C.S.E. subjects or anything else. Whatever does *she* want?" she added as Lettie came padding up the lane towards them, out of breath and bright pink. Comfort wound down the window.

"Cheerio, then," Lettie shouted as Frank Jarrett slowed the taxi obligingly. "See you when you come back ... if you ever do come back." She ran alongside. "Don't forget to write ... and don't do anything you can't do on a bicycle ... and mind you keep your eyes on the road, Frank Jarrett."

For an instant Comfort glanced towards the driving mirror, saw lips parted in a reluctant grin under a tawny moustache.

"That girl," Granny said as the taxi accelerated and Lettie fell behind. "She gets worse all the time."

Comfort looked back where Lettie was still clowning an energetic farewell in the middle of the lane, scissors jumps and arms waving. Then the taxi rounded a bend and all she could see was the distant marshes, squares of green between the straight lines of ditches the Romans had made, stretching away to the shiny line of blue grey sea.

Suddenly Penfold seemed very much her home, the place where she was safe and wanted to be. What had Lettie meant ... *if you ever do come back*, a thread of anxiety twisted round inside her stomach.

Comfort stuck her head out of the window. Was Lettie still shouting, all she could hear was the plaintive call of a peewit down on the marsh ... or it could be a seagull, birds flew everywhere ...

"There's rather a draught, dear," Granny said with one hand held to her fluttering grey curls. "Do you think we could have the window up?"

"Sorry, Granny," Comfort said.

Chapter 4

Bright white light was pecking at her eyelids, Comfort opened startled eyes.

"Efua," she murmured but the air hostess bending over her, newly lipsticked smile and gleaming teeth, was not Efua. Efua no longer flew the Heathrow to Accra route, Mante had told her that. But she had been dreaming about Efua.

"Fasten your seat belt, please. We'll be down in just a few minutes. I think you were being fast asleep, Comfort."

"Sorry," said Comfort. Her mouth was dry and her head full of small discordant noises like the twittering of birds and the squeaking of bats, her legs in jeans were already too hot. "Sorry."

Beyond the window speedwell blue sky and brilliant sunshine. Below a huge expanse of sea, white-topped waves rolling in steady succession from the Atlantic ocean to break upon a pearl-grey beach. Fishing canoes lay like a line of brown earwigs, drawn right up to the wide fringe of palm trees which separated the beach from the flat

39

reddish land behind, stretching away to the scalloped horizon of low green hills.

"Africa. I absolutely can't be disappointed now," Comfort announced in a triumphant whisper, uncrossing her fingers and glancing sideways in case someone had heard her. But there was an empty seat next to hers and the businessman in a beige suit beyond was preoccupied with his seat belt. She had said the same thing silently in her head for the past six weeks, said it with a lift of the heart when the ticket arrived from Mante but almost immediately doubt and hazards crowded in. Tickets could easily be cancelled if something happened just as they had been last year. She had never allowed herself to say it aloud until now. Not when they got to Heathrow, not when Granny had identified her flight number on the departure board and Grandad had secured a trolley and she had seen her luggage disappear along the moving belt. Not even when she had kissed them both and gone through the departure doors because the flight could still be cancelled if there was an engine fault for instance or a bomb was found in a plastic bag.

Waiting in the departure lounge all she could think of was Granny's cheek as she kissed it, unresisting and dry as tissue paper and sunk in against her teeth, blue eyes turned grey as winter puddles.

Comfort had realised at that instant that Granny had been hoping against hope that the ticket would be cancelled. The two of them boxed and coxed like figures on a weather vane. It was infuriating, but what Granny wanted for Comfort would always be the opposite of what Comfort herself wanted. It was sad too, because neither could be happy at the same time. Was Granny hoping even now as Comfort walked along the tunnel to the airplane that both pilots would suddenly get appendicitis or yellow fever, perhaps she had been keeping her fingers crossed when, blinking hard, she said, "Have you got your holiday reading handy for the journey, Comfort? No sense wasting time, just sitting."

"Tess of the d'Urbevilles," Comfort said.

"Goodness me," Granny laughed huskily. "Well, you young girls grow up fast nowadays and I suppose it is literature."

"Mm," said Comfort. She felt a real nit in her green gingham school uniform but Granny had insisted and there was no need for her to know about the jeans packed in her flight bag, ready for a switch."

"I can't be disappointed now," Comfort had thought as the plane roared down the runway and rose like a swan into the violet evening. Below red and green and blue lights flashed and flickered all round the airport like an out of season Christmas tree and then they were soaring upwards and she could see the silvery line of the Thames and then the smaller rivers that ran into it. She wished she knew their names. Granny could recite the rivers of England going right round the entire coast. She had done so only yesterday, the first day of the holidays, while rolling out pastry for treacle tarts, improving the shining hour and Comfort's culinary skills. She would learn the rivers of England and recite them to Granny when she got back as a sort of present, Comfort thought. She could learn all the rivers of Africa too, starting right now with the map in the pocket in front of her. Senegal, Gambia, Tano,

Ankobra, Prasue, Volta Noire, Volta Blanche ... Volta Noire – she preferred the word noire to black, it was sort of soft and innocent sounding. Did they write *Noires, allez vous en* on Paris walls? Rivers carried food and life as well as water. Knowing French and all the rivers could be useful ... if Bob Geldof ever needed a personal assistant for instance.

But that was yesterday and now the passengers were all round her and the plane was down, bumping along the runway and a few moments later as she came down the steps Comfort saw Mante waving from the wide veranda above. He wasn't wearing the white shirt of the photograph but a patterned shirt in blue and yellow local cloth and he looked a little thinner, but his smile was still the same, his wide joyous smile. Then she was tight in the circle of his arms, strong arms thick round as tree branches. She felt his warmth and sniffed his aftershave, freesia-scented, she had sent it for his birthday in a blue and silver box. She could feel the thud of his heart as her cheek pressed tight against his chest.

"Comfort, my daughter, Comfort," he said. "It's good you have come."

"Father," she whispered. She had arrived. Nobody, not even magic or Onyame himself, could take her arrival away from her now; but Mante was talking with his arms still round her, the rumble of his voice like holding your ear to a seashell.

"Comfort, my first born child. *Akwaba*, welcome."

"It's been such a long time," she said.

"Two whole years," said Mante and added, to people waiting in the foyer and the Ghana Airways staff behind their counter, "This is my daughter, Comfort, at boarding school in England. She has come to stay for the school summer holidays." Did he have to tell everybody, Comfort thought, smiling uneasily, but nobody seemed to think such a public explanation odd. She had forgotten how it was in Ghana, how friendly and open, how she had to be a different person. Hadn't she come to find that different person? Besides Efua worked for Ghana Airways and some of these people were probably her colleagues. Comfort's heart gave a sudden lurch as, released from Mante's arms, she found herself staring right into Efua's eyes. Not the real Efua but her photograph used for a Ghana Airways poster, her smile urging the public to fly with them from every side of the foyer.

"Efua? My stepmother?" Comfort said pointing.

"Yes, yes," said Mante. "My wife is very beautiful woman, winning many contests, Miss Takoradi one time, Miss Axim. Naturally she was chosen for the poster, a beautiful woman is always good publicity. I am very proud. Didn't I tell you about it in my letter?"

"I don't think so," Comfort said. Her head was aching now and the eyes in the poster seemed to be watching her wherever she looked.

"I am not the best letter writer," Mante laughed boisterously and all the people round joined in. "Every month my daughter is writing to me from her boarding school at Folkestone, English seaside resort."

"Every fortnight," Comfort muttered.

"Never mind, never mind, now you are here we can talk and talk like a real father and daughter, can't we?" His arm still round her shoulders gave her an affectionate squeeze.

"Mante Kwatey-Jones has *been-to* daughter,"

people were saying all round, everybody seemed to know him. Was it because he worked in the government service that a small retinue had gathered, young men in shorts and singlets, women in cotton dresses or bright clothes patterned with oranges or hibiscus or birds or playing cards.

"Aye-aye, this is my daughter from England," Mante was saying, holding her at arms length and looking into her face. "You have your grandmother in you, Comfort. Anyone can see that. A chip off the old block, isn't it?"

"Aye-aye, this is fine-fine girl. Anyone can see she is twig from Kwatey-Jones tree," somebody said behind them.

"'A tree surrounded by the forest can stand against the wildest hurricane'," another observed. "So it is with family."

"Off we go then," Mante said picking up her case and steering her out into the hot white light of the car park and towards the Airport Hotel. "I expect you'd like a coke?"

Comfort swallowed. "I think I'd rather go straight to the house if you don't mind ... I feel a bit sick."

"Is dehydration," Mante said with a confident sweep of his free arm. "Drink soon fix." The hotel was air-conditioned and pleasantly cool and the followers had dwindled as they crossed the car park. At least she would have his attention all to herself for a few minutes before they went back to Efua.

"Did you drink plenty on the plane ... fruit juice and such?" Mante went on.

"Not much," said Comfort.

"Always drink plenty-plenty and eat as little as possible, then you won't get sickness and jet lag," Mante said.

"Sorry," said Comfort thinking guiltily of dinner served twice and eaten twice during the flight as well as the various snacks. Not that she had been hungry exactly but all the little packages were intriguing and besides with people starving all over Africa it was wicked surely to waste food.

"Jet lag," her father teased. "Is this the girl who sold cloth in the market of Akwapawa? Ata never stop telling me my daughter Comfort is market-clever."

"It's lovely to be here in Ghana again," Comfort said as they sat down and Mante ordered coke. In Ghana people spoke out more, talked about their feelings, displayed their clothes and possessions and admired each other's openly in a way which in England would be considered impertinent or boastful and definitely not-done. Would this be the moment to give him the tie-pin while they were alone together, she didn't want Mante to think she was cold and ungrateful. "I mean the ticket was awfully expensive and everything and I was afraid right up to the last minute that it might be cancelled."

"Cancelled?" Mante said raising his eyebrows. "I am not a rich man, nobody who works for the government is rich nowadays. It is House Cleaning time, the government is saying ... no more dash ... no more corruption ... no more kalabule, black market ... no more smuggling gold ... still, by working night and day, I can afford to pay for my daughter's air ticket."

"I meant ... well ... cancelled like last summer. I mean I know you couldn't help it or anything ..." Comfort stammered. She wanted to please him more than anything but as she spoke the cheerful exuberance went from his face.

"Aye-aye, Efua was very ill last summer," he said huskily, "and the child returned to his sky-family."

"I'm sorry," Comfort said. "Sorry."

"Aye-aye … it was a sad time," Mante said. There were tears in his eyes. "But we must not argue with fate and sad times pass …"

"But Jeo is all right?" Comfort said anxiously. Her head echoed with strange sounds like a child's whimpering.

"Yes, yes, Jeo is a fine boy," her father said, his spirits reviving. He pushed back his shoulders. "And he is looking forward to meeting his sister from English boarding school who sends him woolly lamb for his birthday. He carries Lambkin everywhere he goes. But Jeo takes after his mother's family, of course, it is often so with a first born son. The new child, the baby expected in a month's time, he will be a true Kwatey-Jones, a true Ga."

"It might be a girl?" Comfort suggested but her father's gaze was travelling round the lounge and he did not answer. "Anyway I hope it's not late … I mean I'd like to see the baby before I go back to school, whatever it is."

"Late?" Mante's eyes came back to her. "How late? Here we have modern hospital, best in Africa … with expensive electronic equipment which sees that babies are born at the right time. Our paediatricians command very high fees … as high as anywhere in the world. We do not have old-fangled methods here."

"I just meant …"

"And your school uniform is costing me plenty of money, with special dress for Sunday," Mante said. "Why you do not wear?"

"Well … well I've got it in my flight bag," Comfort

said floundering. How come she got everything wrong. "I didn't know you … shall I change in the Ladies?"

Two women in cloths and matching kerchiefs, dark-blue patterned with white diamonds, and fawn patterned with black pineapples, were coming purposefully across the lounge.

"Greetings and good morning, Mr Mante Kwatey Jones, sir," one of the women said.

"Good morning to you too," Mante said heartily. "And this is Comfort, my daughter, who has just arrived from school in England."

"Aye-aye, a *been-to* daughter," said the woman in the blue cloth. "A big big man like Mante Kwatey-Jones can choose the best schooling in England for his daughter, a school like Eton, isn't it?"

If Mante was irritated by such flattery he did not show it. "We are having plenty of good schools here in Ghana," he said equably. "My daughter was born in England when I was a student there. She is top of the form at her school."

"Aye-aye, 'the fledgling eagle will always soar to the sky'," said the woman in the fawn cloth.

"Well actually …" Comfort murmured.

"A wild rice child," the woman went on. "Such things happen when young men study overseas but Mante Kwatey-Jones does not forget his wild rice daughter."

"Comfort is the child of my first wife," Mante said, slightly irritated now. "What can I do for you, ladies? Please sit down."

"My sister's son, a graduate from the University of Ghana, he is trying to get into the government service," the woman in the blue cloth said pulling up a chair. "And I am saying to my sister, what a

47

young man needs is the help of a big man like Mante Kwatey-Jones, just as the young vine needs the support of a strong tree. Perhaps you could put the right word in the right ear?"

"Like the ear of Jerry Rawlings, our Junior Jesus?" said the woman in the fawn cloth.

"There are no ears in the government nowadays, Provisional National Defence Council does not have ears," Mante said sternly. "Your son must rely on his own merits like the other candidates."

"Very true, very true," the woman said. "House Cleaning time, isn't it? We understand how it is but a young man does not always have the right words. He would like to work for you, Mr Mante Kwatey-Jones, but shy, isn't it?"

"We'll see, we'll see," Mante said relenting, taking an envelope from his pocket and making a note of the name. He smiled across at Comfort as the women got up to go. Comfort smiled back and then yawned.

"Sorry, I didn't sleep much on the plane," she said. "Do you get lots of people wanting you to help them like that?"

" 'When there is a big tree small ones climb on its back to reach the sun'," Mante said.

"Well, anyway, I wasn't top of the form last term," Comfort said. "I was second."

"I was talking about next year," Mante said laughing. "Next year my daughter will be top of the form, that is decided."

"Hadn't we better go home," Comfort said, her coke finished, her fingers playing restlessly with the handle of her case. People had settled at tables on either side and seemed to be trying to catch Mante's eye. "I mean, Efua might be worried."

"My wife does not worry," he said with dignity. "A woman with a good husband has no cause for worry, she prepares the meal and waits for her husband's return."

"Mm," said Comfort doubtfully. Such meekness hardly seemed to apply to Efua unless she had changed a great deal.

"But perhaps it is time we went," Mante conceded getting up. There was a murmur of disappointment from the tables round.

"What about those people?" Comfort whispered as they crossed the hall.

"Your father is a big man in Finance and Economic Planning Department," Mante said smiling and shrugging his shoulders. "Always there are people wanting permits and licences … everywhere I go people are wanting to see me. Everything has changed, you see, now we must encourage new industries, and more people to come from overseas … 'A beggar has no choice.'"

Outside the sun had risen to its glittering zenith and the air was oven hot. Mante spread a leopard skin rug across the seat of the car.

"And Efua is okay?" Comfort asked as they drove towards Hillside Estate.

"She is a little …" Mante took one hand from the steering wheel and rocked it from side to side to complete the sentence. "So many charges at work … a computer installed at Ghana Airways …"

"But I thought Efua liked modern things … new things … Like air-conditioning?"

Comfort said. "Air-conditioning yes, we are air-conditioned now," Mante said. "Me … I do not care for the air-conditioned bedroom. Too cold."

He was silent after that, his eyes slitted against

the glare. Perhaps he didn't like to talk when he was driving, Comfort thought, silent too. Ahead the grey road shimmered with rising heat. It would be easy to imagine that the shining surface was water ahead, a mirage in the desert. A boy herding pale-coloured humpbacked cattle at the side of the road, waved his stick and grinned cheerfully.

Presently they turned off the main asphalt road and reddish laterite dust rose in the cloud round them. She stared out at the low hill and the brown and white square bungalows spread out with plenty of space between on its lower slopes. Each one was built on three sides of a central patio with a high gate and lattice fence on the fourth side.

"Nearly there," Comfort said but Mante still said nothing. His hand on the wheel was tight, his expression tense. Was it something to do with her not being in school uniform, not being top of the form, Comfort wondered. Was he disappointed because she wasn't prettier or more polite.

"I'm so looking forward to seeing Jeo," she said as the silence between them became oppressive. "It's really lovely having a little brother ..." still Mante said nothing. "Be nice seeing Winnie, too." Winnie, the steward's wife, was not much older than Comfort and had been a good friend on her previous visit.

"Winnie doesn't stay at the house any more," Mante said and his frown deepened. "Please do not mention Winnie to your stepmother. I do not want her upset ... with the child so near ..."

"Sorry," said Comfort. "Has there been a quarrel or something?"

"Chu ... " said her father irritated. "What is this quarrel quarrel stuff? We do not quarrel with servants."

"Oh, sorry," said Comfort subdued. People in Ghana seemed so open and cheerful yet it was just as easy to say the wrong thing. Just as many things shouldn't be said and just as many things were not done despite the great Ghanaian heart. It was difficult to work it all out with feeling sick and the noises in her head. The jacaranda tree by the drive was flowering and mauve blossom fell into her lap as the car slid into the garage. John, the steward, stood at the top of the steps in his khaki shorts and shirt.

"Welcome, Comfort," he said smiling. "Master got fine fine daughter. Not pikkin now time. Comfort, she go come fine-fine lady now time."

"Hallo, John," Comfort said shyly. His hand in her grasp felt dry and he seemed to have shrunk a little, the sockets round his eyes were deeply hollowed.

"Where's Missus?" Mante said.

"Missus go out early, take pikkin, take Peace and go drive in car."

"Did she say where she was going?" Mante said.

"No say," John shook his head. He was uneasy, almost frightened, his eyes darted away. "No say where go, no say why go. Missus drive car. *Whoosh.*" His hands shot through the air expressively. From the shade of the garage the three of them stared at the sun-baked drive where tyre marks showed dark in the red dust. Had Efua been angry because she was coming, Comfort wondered. Stepmothers always hated stepdaughters. You could tell that from fairy stories. Chinese fairy stories were the same, Maxine said, full of wicked stepmothers.

"Oh well … you had better bring the chop, man," Mante said.

The living room was cooler, shadowed by louvered shutters closed against the heat of the day. A fan rotated in the ceiling overhead, stirring the air. There was a new table and chairs in the dining end and a new rug on the polished parquet floor. Comfort cut the cold beef into small pieces and covered it with mustard. The burning heat inside her mouth relieved the numbness of her feelings and the ache in her head. Opposite Mante ate in silence. He had phoned Efua's mother and sister, he had phoned the hospital, but nobody had seen Efua or had any idea where she could be.

"Perhaps you should phone the police?" Comfort suggested in a small voice. Granny phoned the police at the smallest mishap or inconvenience. It was her duty to do so and theirs to help her, Granny said, didn't she pay her taxes. "I mean if Efua is really missing."

"Chu," Mantne pushed back his chair impatiently. "A man in my position does not go to the police."

"Well but … I mean … don't they look for people?" Comfort swallowed. Everything she said seemed to make things worse. "Don't they … I mean … don't they find missing persons?"

"My wife is not a missing person." Mante said sharply. "You talk too much for a girl of your age. Here we say, 'It is always the half-full bucket which splashes water most.' Efua has gone to lunch with friends that is all. I daresay she told me and I have forgotten … always I am busy-busy … permit for this one, license for that. Most likely she has gone to Labadi for the day, her friends have a beach hut there." As he spoke his tone had become progressively more cheerful, at least he had convinced himself that there was no cause for alarm.

"I expect that's it," Comfort said flatly, but she didn't believe Efua had gone to any beach.

"She'll be back this evening and we will laugh at all this worry-worry business," Mante said. "But now I must get back to the office. I'll see you this evening, Comfort, have a nice rest now."

Paddington Bear curtains, somewhat faded now, still hung at the windows, and there was brown mosquito netting and outside shutters closed against the midday sun. Beyond she heard the sound of the car driving away, the *whoosh* of the tyres suggested Mante was angry too. The chest of drawers which had been cleared for Comfort was already pollened with today's pink dust. Comfort swept it away with her arm and put her case on top.

Arrived in Ghana, she wrote for July 20th. Six weeks. September 3rd was the date of her return ticket. A little slice of time compared to her previous visit. What a lot could happen in six weeks. *Efua and Jeo gone out.* Her eyes circled the bedroom. Jeo's cot, painted white, lay along the opposite wall under the window which looked into the central patio, Peace's camp bed stowed underneath. The side of the cot was down and the imprint of Jeo's head showed on the embroidered pillow case, one black hair curled like a watch spring, nestled against the lazy daisies and half-concealed by the pillow was Lambkin.

"Jeo?" Comfort whispered picking the woolly lamb up. "Jeo, where are you?"

It was stifling hot and as she lay down to sleep just for a moment Comfort thought of the cool green dampness of Kent. But she was in Ghana now and by this evening Efua would be back and everything would be all right. Probably. But questions still churned in her mind as she sank towards sleep. Why had Efua gone, she wondered guiltily, was it because she wanted to have her father to herself, could Efua know Comfort had wished her gone.

Chapter 5

"Good morning, Comfort," Mante looked briefly over his newspaper. The sun was brilliant already but purple-pink bourgainvillea, clambering up the wooden posts of the veranda, cast a patch of dappled shade where the breakfast table and been laid. The breakfast crockery was new, irregular dark green stripes on white.

"Good morning," Comfort banged the top of her boiled egg vigorously, clowning a bit to get his attention and lighten the atmosphere. She had had his attention, all his attention, last night when they talked but this morning her father's brows drew together in irritation.

"Must you, Comfort?" he murmured.

"Sorry," said Comfort. His moods were as changeable as April showers. Was that why her own moods changed so much? Hereditary. "Is this egg from the Back-Yard-Farm-in-the-City hens?"

"Of course," Mante said. "We are self-sufficient in eggs."

When he came home the previous evening,

Comfort had been waiting. They had eaten together and then sat out on the veranda in the darkness. Efua and Jeo would be back tomorrow, Mante said firmly, staying with friends overnight was something his wife often did, especially since her maternity leave had begun. And then by common consent they had not mentioned the missing pair again. Instead Mante talked about his work, the extra burden of being head of a department, the taxi business which he still owned but which was run by a not-quite-reliable cousin.

The best part, Comfort thought, was that now she was fourteen, he talked as if she would understand. He had never done that before, last time when she tried serious conversation he had laughed and said, "If a little bird talks like a big bird it may hurt itself with the sound of its own voice." But now he told her about the difficult time they had been through, droughts and bush fires had decimated the harvest and a million Ghanaians suddenly sent back from Nigeria, had worsened a severe food shortage. Inflation and the smuggling of gold and cocoa out of the country had bankrupted the economy and with no money for spare parts, lorries and trains had ground to a halt. Bad times indeed but the worst was over now, Jerry Rawlings was back as leader and self-reliance was the key word. Operation-Feed-Yourself had greatly increased the production of rice and maize and Backyard-Farm-in-the City encouraged even the people of Accra to keep chickens and rabbits. Efua had bought six brown hens in the market which clucked and pecked in the servants' yard and were fed by John. Lorries were back on the road and inflation was down but trade was still difficult. His sister, Ata, came every month now to buy what cloth she could in Accra.

Mante talked warily at first, as if expecting contradiction. But then he forgot to be wary and simply talked on and on like a starving man given food, Comfort thought, listening and keeping very still so as not to distract him and spoil the wonder of it; the two of them talking together under the stars with nobody there to interrupt and no sound but the chirp of cicadas and the throb of distant drums in the warm darkness. They had never talked like this before, perhaps they never would again once Efua came back. She would always be there for one thing. Comfort had given Mante the tie-pin then, real gold, shining new from the shop, Grandad had paid half, Granny wasn't to be told. "Beautiful …" Mante had said, blinking rapidly. "Gold goes out of Ghana and my daughter brings it back." Comfort smiled, was it really Ghanaian gold, she wondered.

And Comfort had talked too, telling him about Lodge School and all the rules and not dones and about Ruby who had thrown a bathroom stool and gone forever and all the things that Granny and Grandad Barton would never understand like Suzanne's sister robbed on Clapham Common by a young black and everyone looking at Comfort sideways, whispering behind their white hands. There were more sideways looks when Winston Silcott was convicted of murdering a policeman at Broadwater Farm, as if it was her fault. Not even Maxine understood how she felt but Mante who had lived in London for three student years, Mante understood.

In the end Comfort had had to go to bed

because her head ached and her eyes kept closing without her permission.

"Goodnight, my daughter, don't worry, your stepmother and brother will be back tomorrow," Mante had said quite calmly. But lying in bed she had heard him pick up the telephone and instantly she was wide awake. He made several calls. She could not hear all the words but each call had the same pattern, greetings exchanged, casual enquiries leading inevitably to a lower more intense tone as he asked whether they had seen Efua and Jeo, finally the phone going down.

What was he doing now, Comfort wondered, in the silence which followed. Was he sitting in despair with his head in his hands? Would he like her to go and talk to him? Didn't they say that a problem shared was a problem halved but what if somebody wouldn't admit there was a problem? In the end she had fallen asleep.

"Did you find anything out?" Comfort asked, eyes down as she peeled her well-cracked egg. Beyond the veranda glossy starlings, iridescent blue-black, squabbled in the grapefruit tree.

"Nothing," Mante shook his head. He was dressed in white trousers and shirt ready for the office, the gold band of his watch worn outside his shirt sleeve. "But there is nothing to worry about, Comfort. Bad news travels fast, don't they say, and if they had had an accident we should certainly know by now. There is some misunderstanding. Efua has a great many friends …?"

"You don't think she might have been kidnapped?" Comfort said.

"How kidnapped?" Mante turned on her sharply. "What is this rubbish you are talking? Ghana is a civilised country. My wife gets in the car which I bought her only a month ago and drives off with Jeo and his nurse-girl, does that sound like kidnapped?"

"No but ... well something must have happened," Comfort said.

"You are watching too much television in England," Mante said. "We read of this in the newspaper, young people watching too much television and showing disrespect to parents. Violence and elderly persons mugged in the street. Last week I said, 'I am glad my daughter, Comfort, is at boarding school with all this violence in English schools and children taking drugs and sniffing glue.' I said this to Efua only last week."

"Well, it's not like that everywhere," Comfort began. "I mean we don't have anything like that at Lodge School ... " But Mante had finished his breakfast and was pushing back his chair.

"I must be in my office at eight o'clock," he said glancing at his watch. "Always I am there punctually, it sets a good example for the clerks to follow."

"I suppose I couldn't come with you?" Comfort said in a small voice. She had travelled hundreds of miles by herself but that was enough and she didn't want to be by herself any more. "I mean I promise I wouldn't talk or anything. I can bring my holiday reading. 'Tess of the d'Urbevilles'."

"It wouldn't be right," Mante shook his head. "A government office is not the place for a schoolgirl, Comfort. Besides I want you to listen for the telephone."

"Can't John do that?" She looked away across the vast expanse of space beyond the veranda. Was he ashamed of her, his half-English child, his wild rice child, now he had been promoted to head of the department. He had taken her into his office last time.

"I do not want servants discussing my private affairs," her father said. "This is a family matter."

"What shall I do then?" Comfort said pushing out her lower lip to hide her disappointment.

"You should have a quiet day and rest from your jet lag. John will see to your lunch and I will be back for dinner this evening. Probably Efua will be back too and we shall laugh at all this worry-worry business," he said, smiling as he spoke, but both his words and his smile lacked conviction.

From the veranda Comfort watched the car disappear along the swish road. The next bungalow was some way off, too far to encourage neighbourliness. Citrus trees and red flowered hibiscus dotted the meagre grass and morning mist hovered just above the ground in irregular white patches. Beyond the estate and its bungalows the plain stretched away to a line of low blue hills on the horizon. But you were never really alone in Africa, even now she could hear drumming, though so faint and faraway that it was almost like the beat of her own heart.

"What do you think has happened to Efua?" she asked as John rattled the breakfast things onto the tray. She knew by now it would only fluster him if she tried to help.

"Missus no say," John rubbed one hand across his face perplexed. "Missus go drive plenty times but no say."

"Was it because of me?" Comfort said scraping the toe of her kickers in the pink dust. Everyone knew about stepmothers. "Perhaps she didn't want me to come or something."

"Missus want Comfort, Missus say she want for Comfort to go come plenty-plenty times. Master's pikkin from England, Missus talk-talk for Comfort plenty times." His smile was reassuring and sweet, yet she didn't entirely trust John who had been a servant small boy, big boy, steward since he was ten, and had studied so carefully how to please.

Comfort pulled at the front of the striped tee-shirt which Granny had bought her the day she broke up. "Can't have you going out there looking all outgrown." She ought to write to Granny or at least start 'Tess of the D'Urbevilles' but not just now, she felt too restless. Her headache was better but there were still strange echoes in her head, twangings and the whisper of unknown voices. Where was Efua, she wondered, if it was just the car had broken down, why didn't she get in touch.

Efua and Jeo still not here, she wrote in her diary for July 21st. Suppose Efua never came back. She ought not to think things like that, it would bring bad luck, *Wishing will make it so*. But she wasn't really wishing because she did want to see Efua and she wanted to see Jeo more than anything. It was nice having Mante to herself but that didn't make it her fault that Efua and Jeo had disappeared surely, not now in the bright light of day. In the corner of the veranda something caught her eye. It was the green and white handle of a cup from the new breakfast set. Comfort threaded her finger through. When had it been broken, John swept the veranda nearly every day, he was sweeping now.

In Mante and Efua's bedroom the shutters were already closed against the midday sun and the room was in twilight. The air-conditioning was switched off now but even so the room was noticeably cooler. She stood there for a moment listening to her own breathing and the occasional tap of the broom against the house wall as John swept, coughing now and then in the dust.

A photograph of Jeo in an ornate silver frame stood on the table between the twin beds. He was very like Efua, his eyes had the same reddish-brown tinge and his nostrils the same proud flare. There were two new wardrobes, white-painted picked out in gilt, and matching dressing-table, evidently Efua's with a whole fleet of little pink and white pots with different creams and beauty aids.

The chest of drawers was Mante's, with his ivory-backed brush on top. Comfort slid the top drawer open, her heart was thudding unpleasantly. Ties, handkerchiefs, studs in a leather box and another photograph face downwards, a photograph of herself in an identical silver frame. She had had it taken just before last Christmas, Mante had thanked her for it and said how grown-up she looked. So why had he bought a silver frame for it and then put it face down in his top drawer. She was angry and hurt but was she more angry or more hurt? Was he ashamed of her or what? Comfort planted it on top of the dressing-table and stared a moment and then put it back where she had found it, face down. It was no good trying to change people, Grandad said.

She turned to the wardrobes. Had Efua taken anything with her. It was hard to tell. There were several cases piled on top and inside four blue uniforms with badges, Ghana Airways, and half a dozen cotton dresses swinging on their hangers and giving out a faint waft of the French perfume Efua always used. In the wardrobe were patterned cloths, clean and neatly pressed. It was like the *Marie Celeste,* Comfort thought uneasily, there were no obvious gaps or signs of a hurried departure. The uniforms seemed slightly menacing but wasn't that just because she shouldn't be looking. She shut the wardrobe door abruptly. At Lodge School looking in other people's drawers and lockers was definitely not-done but it was different surely if people were lost. *Wife of Senior Civil Servant Vanishes,* she imagined the headlines, *Mysterious Disappearance of Local Beauty.*

There was a sudden scufffling outside the shutters and then a loud wail. Startled, Comfort pushed the wooden shutters flooding the room with sunlight. As she did so something crashed to the concrete drain below which surrounded the house. A broken saucer. Liquid, almost the colour of blood, had splattered, there were other stains, dried rust-brown on the windowsill itself. A black cat streaked away into the bushes. Efua put palm oil out to keep away ghosts, Comfort remembered that, Winnie bought the palm oil from the shanty village.

"Where's Winnie, John?" Comfort asked. "I want to see Winnie." Winnie had been her friend and mentor when she came out before, Winnie had taught her the Ga Language and a great deal else. Winnie knew all about spells and magic.

"Winnie no stay for Hillside now time," John said. "Missus no want Winnie for Hillside."

"But where is she?" Comfort was impatient. It was why the house seemed so dead. No Winnie meant no visitors, no chatter in the servants' yard, no cloths hung out to dry, no fufu pounded, only the desultory clucking of hens in the pink laterite dust.

"Missus say Winnie can stay in shanty village." He shook his head sorrowfully but without resentment. It meant he had to cycle back and forth every day but he did not question that masters and their wives were entitled to their whims.

"Can I borrow your bike?" Comfort said.

"Master no like. Daddy, he say pikkin can stay in house," John's expression was doubtful. How could he best please both.

"Oh, please, John. Anyway I'm not a pikkin any more, you said so yourself, and I can't stop here all day and Winnie is my friend, the best friend I ever had," Comfort asserted with a rush of warm feeling, at that moment the words seemed true. "I'll give you two cedis for the bike."

"Winnie want see Comfort too," John said smiling uncertainly. "Okay, Comfort go and come back quick-quick or plenty big trouble for John," he rolled his eyes piteously for emphasis. "Lose job."

"Thanks, John," Comfort said. She followed him out across the kitchen patio to the servants' quarters where the Made-in-China bike was kept safe behind a locked door. "Brilliant."

It was a short bumpy ride along the swish road and then the main road was downhill all the way. As Comfort freewheeled down she passed small groups of women walking towards the bus stop with babies on their backs and baskets on their heads. This was travelling, really travelling, she thought with air rushing in her face, really being here in Africa. She had flown hundreds of miles and seen nothing but blue sky and blue sea, but now she was really seeing things. What you saw became part of you and she was part of this landscape too. Each side of the road there were shiny-leaved bushes and clumps of bamboo and small cultivated patches of cassava and yam. Further back were trees, mango and pawpaw and banyan and here and there a towering silver-barked cottonwood. Birds flew up squawking as she passed.

The shanty village was two miles away, a collection of huts spread out under the trees on one side of the road round the single cold water tap. There was more of it than Comfort remembered from visiting it three years ago, as more people left the land and moved towards the town in search of work. Some huts were built from branches and palm fronds gleaned from the surrounding bush. Others were made from broken boxes, originally containing imported goods and still printed with Nestle, Singer and Raleigh, the detritus gleaned from the town. Stray dogs, white with brown or black patches, large-terrier size, roamed the village scratching in the piles of scattered refuse. There was a strong smell of excrement and rotting vegetable. A girl stood with a bucket on her head, waiting patiently for her turn at the tap.

"Do you know Winnie, John's wife?" Comfort asked, breathless and a little shy. The girl stared blankly a moment, unused to strangers, then she smiled and pointed to a nearby hut.

Comfort wheeled the bike across and peered into the dimness of the doorway. For a moment she could not see anything.

"Winnie?" she whispered. "Big Man?"

"Aye-aye, Comfort," Winnie said emerging from the back of the hut, sandals flapping. She hesitated a moment tightening her red and white cloth under her armpits and then flinging her arms round Comfort's neck. "Akwaba, Comfort, you come back. He tell me you come back. Oh, that is good … good." She stood back all smiles. She was taller now, a graceful young woman. A small baby lay in a basket in one corner of the hut and a little girl in a blue dress clutched at her mother's cloth and stared at Comfort wide-eyed.

"Cloth baby is Ofori," Winnie said proudly. "This girl, Akosua."

"And Big Man? Where is Big Man?" Comfort asked.

"Big Man stay with Auntie in Accra now," Winnie said switching to Ga, a more natural language for the discussion of family business. Comfort let the language flow over and found she could mostly understand. "It is the Ghanaian way. This hut too small for Big Man now." Winnie giggled at her own joke but the hut was indeed small, some eight feet square, windowless, the floor hardened earth and furnished with stools, sleeping mats and baskets and an old chair which Comfort recognised as a Hillside throw out. The roof was extended from the hut at one side and provided a place for the kerosene stove on which Winnie cooked.

"You want to sit down, drink cola or orange?" Winnie inquired hospitably pulling a stool for Comfort and taking a can from a large basket in another corner of the hut while Akosua whined and pulled at her cloth.

"You're still trading, then?" Comfort said fumbling at first but finding the Ga words still there in her head and switching too.

"Trade is very good here." Winnie pulled the basket over for Comfort to see. Before she had sold sweets to schoolchildren and for a few weeks Comfort had helped her, but now Winnie had enlarged her business and sold canned drinks, sugar, tea, tins of milk and meat, plastic combs and trinkets, pens and postcards. "Last year was bad but this year is better. The tro-tro bus and the mammy lorries bring plenty of business," Winnie explained.

Some children gathered round the door peering in. "They do not see many girls like you, white girls," Winnie explained shooing them away.

"But I'm not white," Comfort said.

"Light," Winnie shrugged.

"Did you know Efua has disappeared?" Comfort asked. "And Jeo and Peace?"

"Chu," Winnie said pulling Akosua onto her knee. At the mention of Efua her face had become truculent. "He has told me."

"Where could she have gone?" Comfort asked. At one time Winnie and Efua had been friends, gossiping together although they were mistress and servant's wife.

"How should I know?" Winnie said opening her eyes wide." I don't stay at Hillside any more."

"Did you quarrel or something?"

Winnie shrugged. "I don't quarrel with Missus but Missus quarrel with me. She doesn't like Winnie any more when Winnie has two fine babies. Last year when Missus baby come too soon and go back to his sky family, Missus is angry all the time ... spitting like a cobra at me and Big Man ... and when she sees Ofori is coming she sends me away."

"But that's not fair," Comfort said.

"Fair? What is this fair?" Winnie sighed with the irritation of a mature woman at Comfort's inexperience. "Who says fair?"

The two-roomed quarters with their own cold shower and flush lavatory across the paved yard at Hillside Estate, though hardly a palace, had been more comfortable for her growing family than the shabby hut but it was her husband, John, who suffered most of the burden. For a lively young woman like Winnie the shanty village had compensations. Every day she sat under the shade tree and shouted her wares as the mammy lorries came and went. Between times she suckled her baby and bantered with the young men of the village, flashing her large eyes.

"It is not good for him, biking up and biking down, he is tired all the time and coughing …" Winnie said with a dramatic imitation of John's dry cough.

"Do you think Efua has run away because of me?" Comfort said. Her eyes slid awkwardly away from Winnie, circling the hut and resting on the baby. She was able to make out his features now as her eyes got used to the dimness of the hut. He was just like John.

Winnie shrugged. "When Missus baby died she says the first wife's ghost is jealous and has killed the baby."

"But Margaret wasn't like that, wasn't jealous of anybody," Comfort protested. "I mean even if her ghost did come … it wouldn't harm Efua's baby, really it wouldn't."

"Who knows?" Winnie shrugged. "Some say the first wife is always jealous." She had been to school for six years and did not care to argue for magic like a bush woman but surely an ill-wishing ghost was the best explanation for Efua's misfortune, eight years married and only one child safely born.

"Missus didn't want Comfort to come. She wanted to cancel the visit again and when Master wouldn't agree she shouted and threw plates, such a temper, that one." Winnie grinned, evidently she had had a lively description of a recent fracas from John. "Always she is getting new things through Ghana Airways, and then she breaks them."

"Where do you think Efua has gone then?" Comfort said sipping her drink.

"Where?" Winnie said considering it obvious. "Krempepong. The village in Ashanti where she was born, where she can be at peace. There is a lake at Krempepong, they say, a sacred lake. Missus is saying 'It is terrible for an *adehye* woman with royal blood to be married to *omamba*', and Master is saying, 'How can a modern woman talk such old-fangled stuff.' Aye-aye ... Missus is a new-fangled woman but every week Peace comes to the village here for red palm oil to keep away ghosts."

"It's cats which drink the palm oil," Comfort said flatly. Perhaps Efua had put her photo in the drawer because of ghosts. "I've seen cats."

"Maybe cats," Winnie said as Ofori woke in his basket and began to cry. "Maybe ghosts." She scooped him up and let the cloth fall to her waist.

"Do you know this?" Comfort said pulling the woolly lamb from the back pocket of her jeans.

"Lambkin," Winnie said. "Wherever he is Jeo will be crying and crying now without Lambkin."

"You are friends with Peace?" Comfort said.

"Who says friends?" Winnie said pushing her nipple into the baby's mouth. "Peace is Missus' cousin, isn't she, and who can be friends with Ashanti women? Besides she speaks very little English and no Ga," and in case Comfort had not got the point Winnie added, "Ga people like you and me and Master are gentle but Ashanti are fierce, Ashanti always trouble. Didn't the Ashanti cut the head off the big British chief?"

"What chief? When?" said Comfort.

"Oh, long time ago," Winnie said vaguely. "But no one forgets."

Chapter 6

I wish Winnie was living here at Hillside, Comfort wrote in her diary on 29th July and nibbled the end of her pencil. A week had passed since Comfort's visit to the shanty village and John had been reluctant to lend his bike a second time, cedis or not. Comfort had not mentioned the visit to Mante, it seemed better not. She wrote her diary every day now, sitting on her bed and reducing the formless days to small white squares, looking back at what she had written before, day-dreaming. Lodge School seemed less monotonous, the small excitements, fire drill, Suzanne swallowing a plum stone, the day Miss Beale had high-lights put in her hair. Besides you were never alone at Lodge School, couldn't get away from people even if you wanted.

March 20th. *Ruby's gone. Nobody knows where but Estelle says she left in a mini with a social worker in a green hand-knitted dress.* "Have nothing to do with a girl like that," Mante had said sternly when she told him about Ruby which she knew was a mistake.

"Bad girls like that should not be at Lodge School."

"But Ruby's black, isn't she?" Comfort murmured, pouting out her lower lip. "I mean …" What did she mean, that all black girls should stick together.

"There is white trash and black trash too," Mante said. "Are you Jesus Christ or what?" Granny had said much the same thing in different words.

Efua and Jeo are at Krempepong, Comfort wrote. It wasn't just that Winnie had said so, the truth had a way of sounding true. Mante didn't seem all that worried, and as the days passed when he should have been more worried he was obviously less. He had told her to say that her stepmother was away for a few days if anybody asked. Comfort found the village on the map, her eyes drawn instantly by the long oblong of blue, like a bit of river cut off, Krempepong lake. She knew that that was where Jeo had gone – Jeo and Efua and Peace. Mante knew too, but he was too proud to admit that his wife had run away and left no message or perhaps too angry. Ruby breaking windows, Efua breaking cups, awful things happened when people got angry. Mante being angry was shivery cold. Long ago doors slamming in the night, shouting, and Mante gone.

What am I going to do? Comfort wrote. At Lodge School you always knew what to do, the buzzer or Miss Beale or the prefects told you. On the wall above her head Bob Geldof stared into the middle distance. "What shall I do?" she whispered but his vague half-smile suggested no course. Mante had reservations about Bob Geldof. An idealist, yes, he had saved thousands of Ethiopians from starvation but such things were best left to governments, experts in the long run, Mante said. Food aid was addictive like drugs, people, families, whole nations came to rely on it instead of growing food for themselves. Trees cut down and soil eroding everywhere in Africa and less and less food grown every year. Self-reliance was essential for the Third World, Mante said.

Comfort was alone. They said you were never alone in Africa and even now in the late afternoon she could hear distant drumming which pulled at her feet like the tug of a receding wave. Like suburbs anywhere, cars left in the morning and returned in the evening but Hillside itself had changed. As well as the chickens and patches of growing vegetables of Backyard-Farm-in-the-City, there was a general air of shabbiness, peeling paint and stained walls.

Once a woman in a dark blue cloth with matching kerchief tied in a peak, came out of her house as Comfort wandered on the swish road and stood there waiting, tall and stately as the figurehead of a galleon. Two small boys stood behind her.

"You must be Mante Kwatey-Jones daughter?" she said smiling and holding out her hand. "I am Adelaide Boateng from 17, Hillside. Is Efua all right? I haven't seen her for some time."

"She's gone away," Comfort said.

"That must be lonely for you, perhaps you would like to come swimming with us some time?" Mrs Boateng added after a pause. "I take the boys down to Achimota School pool nearly every day."

"But I haven't got a costume or anything," Comfort stammered.

"I'm sure we could find something for you to wear," Mrs Boateng laughed.

"Sorry, I don't like swimming much," Comfort said and walked on abruptly, aware of Mrs Boateng's puzzled eyes gazing after her retreating back.

"Maybe that girl can't swim, Mama?" said one of the boys.

After that Comfort made a detour round 17, Hillside choosing to be alone because anything else was too difficult with too many questions. She had never been alone in Wanwangeri except in her own hut, the hut which Grandmother had given her when her cousin, Ama, became a woman and got her own hut, though Comfort was still under age for this privilege. But even in her own hut the sound of the compound was all round her, children, chickens, *fufu* pounded, the tap of Grandmother's stick.

She wrote letters to Granny and postcards to Maxine and Lettie and Grandmother too. She had sent a picture postcard to Grandmother every month since she left Wanwangeri, shiny sepia kittens with crimson bows, views of Folkestone, ancient churches, what to choose. Now she sent a postcard she had bought from Winnie, the Ambassador Hotel built to celebrate Ghana's independence thirty years ago, a great white building like a palace, though Mante said most of the bedrooms were out of use now because the roof leaked and the so-expensive kitchen equipment did not work any more and the cooking was done in the open at the back. But surely Grandmother would like to see the great Ambassador Hotel.

In the evening Comfort noticed a thin ribbon of smoke coming from somewhere beyond the next bungalow and rising into the pale blue sky. Mante wasn't home yet, no car in the garage, and she set off to investigate. It was cooler now but the fire was further away than she realised, behind the servants' quarters three bungalows away. Tete, gardener for the whole Estate had caught a grasscutter, a large bush rat, and was roasting it over the fire. He had removed the entrails and flattened out the furry flanks spreading them over sticks so it looked like a huge bat. His bloodied knife was still in his hand.

"Oh," said Comfort startled. "What's that?"

"Him good for chop," Tete grinned up at Comfort. He smelt strongly of smoke and sweat, his eyes had a yellowish tinge. "Him grasscutter, good for chop."

"You're going to eat it?" Comfort said and as she watched the flames lick into the brown-grey fur, hundreds of tiny scarlet mites ran towards the temporary safety of the head, desperately crisscrossing on the bald and bony nose of the grasscutter until they pitched off into the fire. Like the flames of hell, the end of the world, Comfort thought, well it was the end of the world for them.

"Very good chop," Tete smacked his lips in illustration, his eyes fixed on her through the haze of smoke. "Nice chop, you want leg?" He leaned forward knife in hand offering to sever it.

"No thanks," she said and ran back then. But she couldn't get the grasscutter out of her head. Was it the scarlet mites and the hundreds of lives or because the smack of Tete's lips reminded her of Frank Jarrett.

"Have there been any phone calls?" Mante's voice came out of the darkness. He was stretched out in his wicker chair on the other side of the veranda. It was not so much a question as a statement because if there had been a phone call she would have run and told him straight away. They both knew that. Besides he had already asked her twice. They had eaten the pork chops, apple sauce and chips which John had prepared, followed by pineapple chunks and now the two of them watched in silence as he cleared the table and carried the lamp inside away from the fluttering moths.

"No, nothing," Comfort said perched on the low wall which edged the veranda. Cicadas ticked in the grass, snakes slithered and small animals ran. There was so much she wanted to know about Africa, Ghana, the Ga, but after the first night their talk had become sporadic and forced. Why hadn't he told her about Efua and Jeo and Krempepong. Would he have told her if she had been all Ghanaian, Comfort wondered. Anger buzzed inside her like a hive of bees but it wouldn't do to talk angry. An ungrateful child was ashes in her parents' mouth.

"Nobody phoned," Comfort added as the silence between them lengthened and a tiny angry voice ticked in her head in time with the cicadas. *Say it, say it now, speak out.* Secrets, things not said, stifled conversation. The trouble was she didn't know how to talk to Mante. She never talked to any man now except Grandad. It was different in the Margaret days, Ferdy at the squat and friends who came to stay and slept on the floor and stayed and stayed. Now she lived in a kind of purdah at Smithy Cottage and Lodge School. From the kitchen she could hear the distant tinkle of crockery and she jumped down wanting to escape. "Shall I help John?"

"No, no," her father dismissed the idea with a wave of his hand. "It is the steward who does steward's work. 'Why keep a dog and bark yourself,' as they say in England." Mante chuckled at the recollection.

"Do they?" Comfort said doubtfully. She had never heard it said and anyway she didn't know anybody in England who had servants. "I thought ... well it's just he has such a long way to cycle home every night."

"He is free to sleep here in his quarters if he wants," Mante said.

"But then Winnie would be all on her own," Comfort said. "I mean the house down there is awfully small and tacky ... Big Man has had to go and live with his Auntie in Accra and he's not even five yet."

"No harm in that," Mante said yawning. "There is much you have to learn, Comfort, about the African way. Children are often looked after by aunts and grandmothers, the greater family. We are not needing orphanage places and old people's homes here." He spoke slowly, lying back and staring up at the stars. "I myself was only five when my mother took me to the mission school and I did not see her for a whole year." He shook his head, smiling wanly at the recollection. "So much crying ... day and night ... night and day ... rivers of tears, rivers of tears ... but now I am an educated man, a been-to with scholarship to England, instead of poor ignorant cocoa farmer."

"Don't you think it was bad for you?" Comfort said, thinking of the weeping little boy. Margaret would have called it cruel.

"How bad?" Mante demanded. "Am I not big man in government office ... a two-carful man ... airconditionful."

"But ..." Comfort began and didn't go on. How could she argue when Mante so disliked argument and crosstalk and more than anything she wanted his approval.

Strains of jazz were coming from the adjacent bungalow and she looked across at the windows. She knew the family by sight now. Black Americans, Mante said resenting them, experts drawn by the high salary and special conditions the government had had to offer. Nothing but their colour was African, birds of passage who had come for their own advantage. Comfort made no attempt to talk to them. They gave her an uneasy feeling of transience, as if she too was not so much staying at Hillside as hovering momentarily like a butterfly.

Her eyes had got used to the veranda without the lamp and she could see her father's face. He was frowning, staring down the length of his long legs in the dark-blue cloth, patterned with yellow birds, which he wore at night. He looked bored rather than anything else and no wonder, Comfort thought ruefully, she hardly ever said anything interesting.

"Did you ... did you have a good day at the office?" she ventured and her voice quavered slightly.

"Much as usual," Mante said and laughed his bubbling thick-honey laugh to show he appreciated her effort. "You sound like a good little wife. Aye-aye ... some days big trouble, some days small trouble but always trouble in this life, my Comfort. Joshua in the office, today he is saying, 'Where did you get that fine gold pin?' 'My daughter,' I tell him, 'she brought it from England.' But you are too much by yourself all day, it is not good for a girl your age." He glanced towards the next bungalow as if it could be expected to offer some immediate solution.

"I'm all right," Comfort said. "Er … are you still working on your book?"

"When do I have time with office business and taxi business and family business?" Mante said. "No one can live on one salary nowadays … and with my wife on maternity leave. But what do you do with yourself all day?"

"Well I write my diary," Comfort said. "And I write letters and I read … and I think about things like … like well, Jeo and Efua disappearing and … and the English chief who was killed by the Ashanti who have never been defeated …"

"English chief?" Mante was puzzled for a moment. "Oh, you must mean Charles MacCarthy, the commander in chief who was killed at Asamonkow, but that was more than a century ago. I write him in my book."

"Yes, him, Charles MacCarthy," Comfort said determined to go on now she had started. "Didn't they cut off his head? And … well … I think about all sorts of things like what is *adehye* …"

"*Adehye* …" Mante paused and looked in her direction. "Where did you hear that word? It means of the royal blood. My wife, Efua, is *adehye*, the granddaughter of an Ashanti chief."

"You didn't tell me that," Comfort said breathlessly. "Why didn't you tell me? I mean I didn't know Efua was Ashanti or *adehye* or anything."

"Such things are not important in the modern world," Mante said.

"Still Efua is *adehye* and Jeo is half-*adehye* and you and me, we aren't?" Comfort said with a little laugh. "We are not that special?"

"We are *omamba*," Mante said. "Ordinary citizens if you like, and proud of it. The Ga are an ancient and cultured people who came to Ghana from Benin hundreds of years before the Ashanti. But, as I say, such distinctions of tribe and rank have no place in the new Ghana, the new world."

"What new world?" Comfort said. Was he talking about Bob Geldof and everybody helping in Africa or what.

"The world we have to live in," Mante said heavily, his eyes stared out into the darkness. "The world which belongs to bankers and economists and industrialists ... the modern world ... Ghana is an independent country, thirty years ago we celebrated getting rid of our colonial masters with much singing and dancing and a hundred fine promises ... I was a schoolboy then, dancing in the street with the others, shouting "Ghana, Ghana for ever" and "Power to the people". But power still lies outside this country. The International Monetary Fund and the World Bank, those people are our new masters, for all we are an independent country we must go cap in hand and beg and plead with them. You must produce this, they say, you must not produce that. You must change your ways, buy this fertiliser for your land, grow cocoa free from disease and green pineapples for export, raise rabbits as well as chickens and cattle, they say. You need foreign experts here to help you, engineers, architects, computer analysts, technicians and you must build hotels for them and the tourist trade and new roads and swimming pools too. Aye-aye, we are an independent country, yes, but we must do what they say."

"Suppose you don't?" Comfort said.

"Then they will not lend us money," Mante said. "It is simple as that. And we need their money. Without it we cannot develop and take our place with other nations, without it we are stuck forever in the Third World. 'A beggar has no choice'." Mante sighed deeply. "It is well said, 'A beggar has no choice'."

"I'm sorry," Comfort said, feeling his distress. "But things are better surely?"

"Better, yes," Mante said. 'We grow more rice, more maize each year … Self-reliance … We must learn to rely on ourselves if we are ever to be truly independent."

"The day before yesterday I went to see Winnie down in the shanty village," Comfort said. "And Winnie says …" she took a deep breath, she had started to say what she wanted and once you started you had to go on. "Winnie says Efua has run away to Krempepong because of me coming … because she doesn't like the modern hospital and wants to be with her own people."

"Winnie says … Winnie says … do you think I care for the talk of servants?" Mante demanded angrily. "Chu, what is this own people stuff? I am her husband, I, Mante Kwatey-Jones, I am her own people and the father of her child. If Efua has gone to Krempepong to stay for a while and taken Jeo, that is her business and mine. Did Winnie also tell you when Efua would come back?" he added sarcastically.

"Of course not," Comfort stared down at her kickers. "She talked about the Ashanti, that's all, how they were fierce and loved fighting and always won in battle …"

"And is this what they teach you at this so expensive boarding school with elocution lessons and special dress for Sunday, to listen to the gossip of servants?" Comfort shook her head. "And I suppose Winnie also told you how we quarrelled and broke cups and plates? Well, you are old enough to know that married people do quarrel sometimes, Comfort, it is nothing so serious." Mante stood up. "This evening I shall work on my book, there is need of it, a history of the Ga People, I can see that …"

At the study door he turned. "As to the Ashanti, they were certainly a fierce people but they are not Gods and they have been defeated scores of times … Dodowa … did Winnie tell you about their great defeat at Dodowa … and Kumasi their capital city burned to the ground, did Winnie tell you that?" He took a book from the bookcase and dropped it into Comfort's lap. "Here, read this …"

That night Comfort was restless, reading and dreaming. The darkness itself seemed restless, cicadas in the grass under the window and swarms of winged termites thudding against the mosquito screen of Mante's study drawn by the light, and behind it the typewriter clicking. What she had said about *adehye* and *omamba* and the Ashanti being undefeated might have annoyed him but at least it seemed to have revived his desire to work on his book. Far away the drumming went on and on.

At last Comfort slept but her sleep was restless too. She dreamed of searching down a long dark corridor. Notices on the walls, "Efua is Not Here", and "Jeo is Not Here", and on and on to Asamankow was it or perhaps Kumasi. Warriors pounding their drums, Ashanti warriors, tall men wearing leopard skins, gold chains at their necks and knees; each chain hung with little bells that rang as they danced. A cannon roared and flashed making the battlefield bright as day and Comfort sat up startled.

"Are you asleep, Comfort?" Mante said standing in the doorway. Sandalled footsteps dragged on the concrete in the darkness behind him. "A surprise for you, Aunt Ata is here. Come and greet your Aunt Ata from Wanwangeri."

Chapter 7

"Aye-aye ... enough cloth for two months," Aunt Ata said leaning back in her chair and laughing the deep bubbling laugh which seemed to come from her whole body, the laugh that was so like Mante's. Ata had always laughed a lot except for the time when her son, Bolo, died. Comfort had never known anyone who lived her life with such gusto. It was late afternoon two days later and Ata arriving back from Accra in a taxi, had called to John and Comfort to help her carry the cloth inside. Now it was piled up in the corner of the sitting room, the brilliant blues, greens, reds and golds gleaming in the light of the setting sun.

"Bring tea at once, John," Ata called extending herself wearily in the easy chair. Her own cloth was black with crimson parrots, a new cloth Comfort had never seen, Aunt Ata always liked to wear the latest fashion. "My throat it is dry-dry with dust," she coughed expressively and rubbed her hand across her face. "Aye-aye ..."

"Anyway you got plenty of cloth," Comfort said.

Her hand stroked the pile of cloth professionally, loving the feel to it. The restlessness was back, old patterns, new patterns, would she like to be selling cloth in the market at Akwapawa like Ata and Esi, Comfort wondered, imagining the shouts of sellers, the shuffle of feet, the clank of buckets, high pitched chatter and infectious laughter. In Africa they starved and suffered so and yet they laughed more than people anywhere else, at home in the world like fish are at home in the water. Suppose she had stayed, would she be part of that laughter now, Comfort wondered.

"Did you pay a good price?" she asked pouring tea.

"Middle-middle," Ata said rotating one hand back and forth with a tinkle of bracelets to illustrate her point and accepting her cup of tea with the other. She spoke a highly individual mixture of English and Ga. "But at least I am having something to sell now."

"You used to buy cloth in Kumasi?" Comfort said.

"Nothing is so easy nowadays," Ata said. "Aye-aye … it is hot down here … too hot," she sighed leaning back and closing her eyes.

"Yes," Comfort agreed pulling the front of her tee-shirt away from her skin, sweaty with carrying cloth. Beyond the veranda at the back of the bungalow the sun was already going down, pinking all the sky she could see. Too much pink she thought suddenly, remembering rhododendrons at Kew. Once she and Margaret had visited in early June, agreeing there was too much pink. Looking back at Ata she was surprised to see a bright gleam under her lowered lids. Aunt Ata was watching her.

"Your Grandmother sent you an amulet with her

greetings," Ata said a moment later. She sat up pulling at the cloth at her waist where she kept her money. "Here, Comfort, I am forgetting to give it to you. It will bring you good luck and a safe journey."

"Journey?" Comfort murmured. She felt her heart quicken taking the amulet, a small leather pouch attached to a loop of leather thong. Inside was a white cowrie shell. She glanced at Ata anxiously, did she remember the amulet Comfort had given to Bolo just before he died, too late perhaps for any benefit.

"Thank her, will you?" Comfort said. "Thank my grandmother for the amulet. Tell her … tell her I'll wear it always." She clutched at the ring round her neck. 'Comfort Jones you have a long way to go,' Margaret had said, she always thought of Margaret when things were changing.

"Why not thank her yourself?" Ata suggested opening her eyes wide. "Come back to Wanwangeri with me for a while."

"Wanwangeri?" Comfort swallowed. She wanted to be with Aunt Ata, she felt her spirit growing and expanding like a seedling in the sun in her warming confident presence. But did she want to see Grandmother who got so angry so quickly, striking out with her stick quick as any leopard? And did Grandmother want to see her? "But … but what about Jeo … suppose Efua and Jeo come back?"

"Efua and Jeo have gone to Krempepong," Ata said firmly. "They will not be back until the child is born."

"But … but I mean she's booked in at the big new hospital … it's all arranged," Comfort said. "Mante says …"

"Chu," Ata said. "Hospitals are man's business, babies women's business, women must choose where the child is born. It is not so special, plenty of women go back to their own village for babies born. Go back to their roots."

"Roots?" Comfort said mystified. Black Americans and West Indians came back to Africa looking for their roots, the chain of family arbitarily broken when they were captured as slaves, but what had roots to do with Efua who had never left Ghana.

"Roots, roots," Ata repeated. "Hospital all white and cold, no songs, no dancing, no wise woman. Machine say baby born today … tomorrow … next week …" Ata shuddered. "I am not liking those places. Are you coming to Wanwangeri where Grandmother is waiting to see you?"

"I don't know …" Comfort said. It was what she wanted. Wasn't she looking for her roots too, she wouldn't find them in the new bricks and mortar of Hillside Estate. "I'd like to but … have you asked my father, I mean he'll be left on his own."

"We ask him tonight," Ata said. There was something calm and inexorable about the way she spoke, as if it had already been decided even before Mante got home. Aunt Ata was a market mammy and market mammies were powerful, *bottom power* it was called, no ruler lasted long without their support. Grandmother was a strong woman, too, and Grandmother and Ata both wanted Comfort to go to Wanwangeri, automatically Comfort went to the bedroom and her hands began to gather the things she would need into a bundle. She would leave her case at Hillside, a case was just a nuisance at Wanwangeri. Since Aunt Ata arrived, Comfort had been sleeping on Peace's small camp bed. Now she stood by Jeo's cot, the imprint of his head on the blue organdie pillow was just as it had been the day she arrived. Carefully she picked up the tiny curl of hair between finger and thumb and put it inside the amulet round her neck. Now perhaps it would bring Jeo good luck too, give them both a good journey and a safe return. She plumped out the pillow making it ready.

"How much? Aye-aye ... my sister is business-clever, all the women in my family are business-clever, eh, Comfort?" Mante said admiring the pile of cloth that evening, calling in a louder tone. "Bring chop, John."

"Yes, Master, go coming, sir," John called back from the kitchen. A moment later the phone rang, Mante disappeared into his study and closed the door.

"Better not wait," Ata said sitting down where John had already put chicken and groundnut stew and rice on the table. They could hear an occasional muttered monosyllable through the study door, when Mante sat down at the table his expression was baffled and angry.

"Cousin of the Asantehene, paramount chief of the Ashanti people is ringing me," he said huskily and suddenly he rounded on Ata and burst out furiously, "What for these people humbug me? What I do wrong, eh? Best gynaecologist ... best hospital ... best private room ... what I do wrong eh?" Red-rimmed eyes glinted angrily. "You tell me why my wife go back to Krempepong and mud hut and make me laughing-stock ... you tell me?"

"Nothing, nothing ... you did everything right,"

Ata said soothingly. "This woman, this Ashanti princess lady big trouble, we are telling you from the start, your mother and sisters are telling you ..." Her voice died away, finding the discussion in front of Comfort unseemly. In the darkness cicadas ticked, bush rats scrabbled, but on the veranda no sound but the click of cutlery on plate and as the silence deepened into awkwardness, Comfort said breathlessly, "My Grandmother wants me to go back to Wanwangeri with Aunt Ata but I'll stay here if you want me to."

"No, no ... you should go to Wanwangeri, of course," Mante said. "The child belongs to the whole family and there is nothing for you here with my wife away. So go with Aunt Ata and give my greetings to my mother. Tell her I will visit soon."

In the morning Comfort got up while it was still dark. Aunt Ata wanted to catch the early tro-tro bus and get to Akwapawa with the new cloth while the day was still cool.

"Wear your school uniform, let my mother see," Mante had instructed the night before. "How can I pay for sister's children's school books when I have Lodge School uniform to buy with special dress for Sunday?" The whites of his eyes moved in the darkness. Was he frightened of Grandmother too, Comfort wondered. It didn't stop her feeling stupid wearing Lodge School dress and blazer in the middle of Ghana.

She put Lambkin in her blazer pocket and stood in the door of Mante's bedroom listening to the rhythm of his breathing like a purring cat and hoping he would wake.

"Goodbye, my father," she whispered. There was

a pause in the breathing, a slight hiccup and a movement of lips and then the rhythm was resumed. He had said goodbye and farewell properly the night before.

"Come," Ata said, already walking away towards the swish road with her sandals Flip-flapping and the bundle of cloth on her head. A line of pale grey sky showed on the horizon now, edged with lemon yellow. They had divided the new cloth the night before and Comfort had practiced carrying her smaller load and her neck felt stiff already. She twisted the kerchief making a round pad for her head and hoisted up her own load of six bolts. Her body had come from Margaret according to Mante but her strong neck must be Ghanaian surely, she thought, as she followed Ata.

Comfort had been in Ghana for more than a week but it wasn't until she saw the tro-tro bus approaching, brightly lit like a little ship on a wide black sea, that she felt she had really arrived. Behind them women with baskets of oranges and tomatoes and men on their way to work in shops and offices shuffled aboard and sat diminished into silence by the early morning start. A chicken with its legs tied together, squawked and struggled intermittently under the seat behind.

The shanty village was already bustling with passengers in transit and mammy lorries coming and going. It was beginning to get light. Would she be able to say goodbye to Winnie, Comfort wondered, but each lorry had a *bookman* touting for custom as well as a driver and, as they alighted, a bookman seized Ata's cloth shouting, "Where you want to go? My lorry good for that place, my lorry go come plenty quick-quick.

"Aye-aye, you good business man for true," Ata protested cheerfully, slipping into pidgin. "Aburi, we want and that next lorry, go come plenty quick-quick." But the bookman had already flung the bolts of cloth onto the roof and was fastening them down. Ata shrugged her broad shoulders respecting his initiative. "Make sure you tie safe-safe. Don't want to lose my cloth business as well as my money." She laughed then, the deep resonant laugh that made Comfort smile, warming her like sunshine. The mammy lorry was painted in two shades of blue, Oxford and Cambridge, Comfort thought, and quickly dismissed it as inappropriate, blue as Krempepong lake in sunlight and shadow. *Suro Basia*, the motto on the bonnet read. She frowned puzzled for a moment and then, remembering, *Fear Women*. The bookman didn't seem to.

"Look, the next one's going first, it's full already," she said nodding towards the orange lorry alongside with the motto *Beggar Has No Choice*.

"*Suro Basia* go first okay," the bookman had insisted but as the orange lorry pulled away he changed his protest to, "Him no good driver, *Beggar Has No Choice*, no good driver."

"This lorry is having plenty of room," Ata said spreading herself generously along the seat and loosening her cloth at the waist for greater ease and wiping her hot face on its edge.

"Tell me about Ama, how she is?" Comfort asked when five minutes later *Suro Basia* moved out onto the road with much revving of engine and clamour of goodbyes. Ama, Ata's daughter, had been her particular friend as well as cousin and 'sister' on her last visit, but though Ata had given news of everybody else she had seemed reluctant to talk of Ama.

"Ama has a fine-fine son, Kofi," Ata said, but there was something constrained in the way she settled her shoulders. "She is living at Preko's village now."

"I expect you miss her and she misses you?" Comfort said politely. "Does she go to the market still?"

"Not much," said Ata yawning and closing her eyes. "She has a child to care for now." But Ata had always had children to care for, Comfort thought puzzled, and it had never stopped her going to the market.

The road rose steadily and soon there was forest on either side interspersed with small patches of cultivation, cassava, yam, okra and peppers, a hundred different greens, leaves as dark as holly and light-bright as larch in spring. The sides of the lorry were open and the morning air was cool, Ata pulled her cloth round her shoulders shawl-like but did not open her eyes. Looking back Comfort could see the wide expanse of the Accra plain, grass thin as bristles on the back of a large red pig, it stretched away to the palm trees fringing the shore and the wide white line beyond where huge breakers rolled in from the Atlantic.

Directly below, the ground fell steeply away and Comfort looked down on the tops of trees, flat like a blue-green cushion and swathed in early morning mist, mysterious. But it wasn't just the landscape that was mysterious, Comfort thought, glancing at Aunt Ata's closed eyes, people were mysterious too. And Grandmother, when Comfort imagined meeting Grandmother again for the first time, a frisson of anxiety tightened her stomach. But it would be different now. She was two years older for one thing and knew much more like ... Like the rivers of Africa and French irregular verbs and how to dissect a frog and the top twenty and Bob Geldof and ...

At Aburi they had to wait nearly two hours for the lorry going in their direction to fill up with passengers. Ata bought orange drink from the stall and sat in the shade to laugh and gossip with other market women in transit, tales of babies born, girls married, land or business gained or lost. Was it because she was half-English and been-to that Aunt Ata didn't talk freely to her like this, Comfort wondered. The people round them looked thinner, shabbier, legs patched with pink open scores which healed to grey. Many children had navels which stuck out from their bellies like hillocks, umbilical hernia, Mante said, caused by village midwifery. Would Efua's new baby have a hillock like that. And what about Jeo. Were his legs already patched with sores.

It was midday when they reached Akwapawa, and the sun was high and hot. Ata, disinclined to set out for the two miles walk to Wanwangeri, bought soup and roasted plantain from the food-sellers. This time she avoided companions and settled in a patch of shade. After they had eaten Ata spread her cloth, made sure her money was secure at her waist, settled her head on the cloth load and was soon asleep.

Comfort lay down, too, staring up at the filigree of palm trees above her head and the tiny bits of blue sky beyond. It was like this in Ghana, she thought, perhaps all over Africa. People lived wholly in the now, the passing moment, making the most of it. Was it something to do with Ghana or something to do with being black. In England the passing moment hardly seemed to exist. At Smithy Cottage Granny was always preparing one meal with her hands but deciding on tomorrow's meal with her head, and even in the garden Grandad trimmed his Albertine or planted stocks but dreamed of the wonders of next year's seeds. At Lodge School you were always preparing for your next exam, already all the heads in her form were set towards G.C.S.E. like racehorses set at the high hurdle. Beyond were further hurdles in endless succession.

Comfort sighed at the prospect and closed her eyes. Suppose she had stayed in Ghana as Grandmother wanted, she wondered as she slid towards sleep. Suppose.

When she awoke it was to the sound of running water. Ata was drinking and washing her face at a nearby standpipe, blowing and bubbling like a dolphin into the flow of cold water. She carried a tin cup of water back to Comfort. The sun had slid from its glittering zenith and was halfway towards the horizon and a slight breeze disturbed the tops of the trees.

"Does my grandmother really want to see me?" Comfort said brushing sand from her blazer. "I mean ... I ran away, didn't I?" To her English self this didn't seem so very serious but as her Ghanaian self began to emerge it was becoming increasingly heinous. "She wanted me to stay, I was to be her eyes and ears ... but I needed my own eyes and ears and I ran away."

Ata tightened the cloth round her waist. "'The

chicken stays on the ground but the fledgling eagle soars into the sky',," she observed sadly, her own eagle-child, Bolo, was dead and her other children most decidedly earthbound chickens. "Come, we must get to Wanwangeri. Grandmother is waiting for the cloth and expecting you."

"Expecting me?" Comfort said. "Did you phone or something?"

"No phone in Wanwangeri," Ata said. "Your grandmother listens to the talking drums, she learns all she wants to know … and other things too, things she would rather not know," Ata added as an afterthought. She swung her load onto her head and moved slowly down the sandy track which was the only road to Wanwangeri and Comfort followed.

Children were waiting at the entrance to the compound and as Comfort stopped inside the woven palm-frond fence, they crowded round. A dozen small wide-eyed children, round-bellied and temporarily awed into silence by Comfort, their been-to sister, visitor from another world and almost a stranger. If the compound itself seemed a little smaller, the children were all taller and somewhat thinner. The older boys, Tete and Ofori had gone now, initiated into their father's *asafo*, the secret society of his clan, and living in the men's house. But two new children had filled the gap, Esi's still a cloth baby and Ata's a sad-eyed boy, Kwashi, two years old and born soon after Bolo died. Tawia, who had been a small girl before, scarcely distinguishable from the other children, now had a different air having taken Ama's place as the big girl, fetcher of water, minder and boss of the little ones.

"Greetings, Comfort, and welcome," Aunt Esi

said smiling warmly.

"Come to your hut," said Tawia in Ga as the little ones began to overcome their shyness, one small hand pulling at the braided edge of her green blazer, another burrowing into her pocket.

"Stop that," Tawia shouted and the children fell away grinning and giggling and dancing out of reach of her flailing slap. "Your hut is just as you left it. Let me show you."

The plastic stripes in bright colours which covered the doorway of Comfort's red hut had faded to the colour of string. Comfort stepped inside and they swished into place behind her, shutting out the yellow evening sunlight. Inside the hut was just as she remembered, the walls reddish and crumbly to the touch, the roof shadowy, the roof poles which held up the thatch dotted with the mud nests of wasps. Her striped suitcase much ravaged by termites lay in one corner, baskets hung from the several hooks in the walls, the sleeping mat was propped in one corner but there was a bed as well now, freshly made of new wood, and shiny with yellow varnish.

"Grandmother got Taro, the carpenter, to make it," Tawia said holding back the flock mattress to show the slatted wood underneath, a trace of fresh sawdust trickled to the hard earth floor. "Last week when she knew you were coming."

"How could she know?" Comfort murmured, the matter had only been decided the night before.

"Oh, Grandmother knows everything ... well nearly everything," Tawia corrected herself carefully. "She knew you would come back ... she always knew."

"Well ... but I'm not staying long," Comfort said

quickly. "Only a month, I've got to get back to school." Was it her fatigue or the tantalising smells of cooking coming from the compound and all the village round, blue smoke rising to the evening sky, which made her words sound so unconvincing, as artificial as a doily.

"Oh, school," said Tawia sitting herself gingerly on the new bed beside Comfort and expanding her chest to enhance the small marshmallows of her developing breasts. "I shan't go to school after next year. I have too much to do, fetching and carrying and cooking and looking after all the children and Grandmother."

"And Grandmother, she is well?" Comfort inquired glancing involuntarily over her shoulder.

"Oh, yes, she always sleep all the afternoon," Tawia said adopting a grown-up tone. "It is not wise to wake her when she might be dreaming and her spirit walking from her body because it might not get back. I am taking good care of your farm, would you like to see it?"

"Oh, yes," said Comfort. Her neck was aching from the two mile walk with the unaccustomed load but she wasn't going to admit it.

"We are going to the farm," Tawia called to Esi, her mother. The children had already gathered round the hearth for the evening meal. They sat in a solemn circle, drawn by their hunger and the smell of food. "Better you stop here," Tawia said as one or two seemed inclined to come with them.

The farm was at the edge of the village and both smaller and neater then Comfort remembered, the bright green leaves of cassava and sweet potato and the pawpaw tree towering twelve feet tall and hung with yellow-green pawpaws as big as vegetable marrows.

"See this cocoyam, it grows wild in the forest but I dug it up and plant it here for you. I take good care of your farm, don't I? Grandmother makes me do that but she don't let me use your hut, not even until you come back." Tawia stuck out her lower lip. "Wait till you are a women, that is the custom. 'Can a bird fly before it has grown feathers?'" Tawia said in a creditable imitation of Grandmother's voice. "But then there was the trouble with Ama and she went to live in Preko's family, so now I have her hut."

"What trouble?" Comfort said crumbling the reddish soil between her fingers.

"Oh, Kofi got scalded with boiling water and Preko's family was very angry," Tawia said widening her eyes and enjoying telling the tale. "Sika says our family must pay money to Preko's family ... Grandmother was very angry and after that Ama went to live in Preko's family."

"What about poor little Kofi?" Comfort asked.

"Oh, he's all right except for this scar on his leg, all white and sort of shiny," Tawia wrinkled her nose in distaste. "Such a fuss. Children get scalded with water or burnt by the cooking fire all the time in Wanwangeri, until they learn to be careful."

Aunt Ata met them at the entrance to the compound. "Your grandmother has woken. She is asking for you, Comfort."

The plastic strips on Grandmother's doorway had been renewed and quivered red, blue and green in the evening breeze. "Can I come in, Grandmother?" Comfort whispered. Her heart was thudding and the palms of her hands felt damp.

"Akwaba, Comfort, welcome," Grandmother said

huskily. She sat on a stool just inside with her stick between her hands. As the strips fell back in place behind Comfort and her eyes got used to the dim light, she saw that Grandmother's face was older, more shrivelled but her eyes were bright and keen as they had ever been. "Greetings, Comfort, so you come back to me. Onyame is good."

"Yes, Grandmother, I have come back," Comfort said using the more formal Ga she had learned from Mante. "I promised, didn't I? I said I would come back? But only for a little while, I have to go back to school in a month."

"School?" Grandmother frowned.

"Lodge School in Folkestone. This is my school uniform, Mante said to tell you we have a different dress for Sunday as well," Comfort's voice was breathless and quavery, but she hurried on. "He says he will visit you soon."

"Aye-aye," Grandmother murmured, Mante's messages hardly seemed to have intruded into her thoughts. "I knew you would come, Comfort. We are the same blood, you and I."

"Yes, Grandmother," Comfort said and her eyes circling the hut saw the wall behind Grandmother's stool was covered with the postcards threaded onto string. They hung flat against the wall in a large square, ancient churches in sepia, views of Penfold, a dozen bright blue views of Folkestone, kittens with crimson bows.

"You look at my postcards?" Grandmother said, tilting her head to look at them too. "I have no window in my hut, I am too poor for windows. These postcards are my window to the world." She smiled as she spoke, her clawlike fingers stroked vaguely at the shiny blue sea at Folkestone. "Does my been-to granddaughter send me postcards?"

"You know I do, Grandmother," Comfort said. "I send them every month from school."

"School?" said Grandmother shaking her head testily. "What is this talk of school? Hasn't your womanhood come to you?"

"Yes," Comfort stammered. "But in England I still have to go to school until I'm sixteen."

"My daughters read and write and add up cedis and that is enough … enough for any woman." Grandmother's eyes were like little black stones.

"Not for me," Comfort swallowed, her mouth was dry. "My mocks next term and my G.C.S.E. and …" she floundered to a standstill. It was as if she was drowning and couldn't speak, drowning and paralysed by Grandmother's powerful will. Her hand clutched the ring at her neck. 'Comfort Jones, you have a long way to go,' Margaret whispered in her head. "You see … I am going to be something." Comfort struggled on. "I mean I might be something like … Like … well a brain-surgeon." But brain-surgeon had only been a joke, she knew that.

"Brain-surgeon, what is brain-surgeon?" Grandmother said.

"A person …" Comfort's voice was high and quavering and she wasn't even sure she knew. "A person who cuts holes in people's heads …"

"A person who cuts holes in people's heads?" Grandmother said wonderingly. "What wickedness is this? What foolishness? Fetch my food at once, Comfort, I cannot listen to such nonsense."

Chapter 8

"Are you asleep?" Tawia's head poking through the strips at the doorway looked like the head of a small animal pushing through grass. Her head was followed by two hands holding up four small empty tins. "For the legs of your bed," she said coming into the hut and letting the strips swing back into place behind her. "Aunt Ata says you must put each leg in a tin and fill with kerosene or termites eat your bed."

"Okay," said Comfort.

"And you must wash as soon as you leave your sleeping bed or you get bad luck all day," Tawia insisted bossily. Her eyes bright with curiosity, circled the hut. "That is the custom."

"I know," said Comfort watching sleepily as her small cousin walked round the bed putting a tin ready by each leg and using the occasion as excuse to study at close range this strange been-to 'sister' with skin light-brown as the thatch on the roof, who flew the world like a bird and wore flowered pyjamas at night, a too-short school dress by day and spoke Ga so clumsily.

"Who's that?" Tawia gazed at the poster somewhat creased now which Comfort had carefully impaled by its corners on the wall hooks the night before. Home was where Bob Geldof was. "Are you his calabash?" Tawia giggled a bit, knowing the word was cheeky.

"Calabash?" Comfort was puzzled.

"Girl-friend," Tawia said opening her eyes wide. How could Comfort travel so far and not know that?

"Course not," Comfort said crossly. Would she like it if she was, she wondered, those eyes and prickly chin so close.

"Well … well anyway I put the bucket of water in the wash place for you," Tawia finished. Aunt Ata was calling, and, unable to delay her departure any longer, she skipped out through the doorway.

Comfort stretched and sat up. Her neck was stiff and aching but she had slept long and deeply in Tako's newmade bed. The early clanking of buckets as water was fetched from the central tap and the protesting wails of children vigorously bathed and rinsed in cold water had not woken her. For a moment she listened to the day-time sounds of Wanwangeri, the thump of *fufu* pounded at the cooking place, snatches of chatter and laughter, the infinitesimal ticking of insect life in the roof above, the gargle of chickens pecking in the dust round the door, feeling as well as knowing she was back.

Ten minutes later Aunt Esi put a small bowl of *garri* left from the night before into her hands. The evening meal, however meagre, was eaten formally and in silence, sitting in a circle, hand dipping into the central bowl of food according to age, eldest first. But breakfast was eaten casually according to what there was and often not taken at all.

"Greetings, my Comfort," Grandmother said, her expression making it clear she was prepared to forget their initial unfortunate meeting. Her stool had been put outside on the concrete apron in front of her hut, the better to see the newly-purchased cloth which Ata and Esi were displaying, holding the long lengths against their bodies, red, green and blue glowing brilliant in the sunlight.

"Aye-aye ..." Grandmother murmured examining each bolt, letting the cloth run through her fingers, testing the quality, clucking softly at the familiar patterns of birds and flowers, crowing with mock horror at the new and daring ones, replicas of newsprint and computer print-out, playing cards, jet airplanes and even portraits of Jerry Rawlings himself. The children shining with soap and cleanliness sat in a ring round the concrete following the proceedings and echoing Grandmother's sighs and exclamations of pleasure and dismay with little pantomimes of their own. Each child had one of Comfort's felt pens tucked behind each ear.

"Aye-aye, you have done well, Ata," Grandmother said when the display was finished and Esi ready to depart to Akwapawa market with her cloth baby on her back, several bolts of new cloth on her head and two small daughters trailing behind.

"Come, Comfort," Grandmother said getting on her feet with some difficulty and leaning heavily on her stick. "Today we will walk through Wanwangeri. Let everyone see that Onyame is good to an old women who keeps the custom, that my granddaughter has come back to me."

"Yes ... well it's only for a month, isn't it?" Comfort said in a small voice. She had talked to Mante before she left to make quite sure her visit to Wanwangeri was only for a month at the very most and to say it and keep on saying it even if Grandmother didn't like it. But Grandmother only heard what she wanted to hear and she gave no sign of hearing Comfort. Instead she flicked the edge of her striped cotton skirt with her stick. "Too short ..." she said.

"Well, it is last year's but Granny thought ..." Comfort began, wanting to be fair but stopped. What had Granny's point-of-view to do with Wanwangeri? "Well, anyway I could wear my school dress if you like?"

"Chu ... school dress ... choose one of the new cloths," Grandmother commanded with a wide sweep of her stick. "Ata can sew for you. A modest young woman keeps her secrets and does not show her legs to all the young men of Akwapawa."

"Mm ... well ... thank you," Comfort murmured. What would Grandmother say to her gym shorts? "I rather like that one," she pointed to a cloth with yellow sunflowers on a dark crimson ground.

"Fine-fine cloth," chorused the children with smiles of approval and much waving of hands. "Very good cloth." She was part of the family already, Comfort thought happily, touched by the way even the children accepted her at once and yet she was not quite part. Their eyes observed her different clothes and the different shade of her skin, perhaps, but what could they know of her different thoughts.

"You choose well, Comfort," Grandmother said thoughtfully. "Yellow is for wealth and property, red is for war, yellow and red together are for the power of life. Come ... let us walk."

The two of them proceeded slowly out of the compound with Grandmother leaning on her stick and holding Comfort's shoulder. And though she leaned more heavily than before she herself seemed lighter, her hands and wrists more bird-like thin and walking more effort. The children followed, dressed in a motley assortment of tattered shorts or cloth twisted round waists or necks, keeping discreetly out of stick range.

From far away the sound of drumming came through the clear blue air, only just perceptible.

"Do you hear the talking drums?" Comfort murmured.

"I hear them," Grandmother said. "But the message does not come from Krempepong ... Ashanti land is that way, that is where the child will be born." She pointed westwards with her stick. How far was it to Krempepong, Comfort wondered, twenty kilometres perhaps. She was nearer to Jeo than she had been at Accra and yet so far.

"Have you seen Jeo?" she asked.

"Once," Grandmother's lips tightened. "The flying-in the-air woman brought the child to visit once."

"Mante says the Ashanti are fierce people who love fighting ... "

"Fierce ..." Grandmother savoured the word. "There are many round here have a few drops of Ashanti blood." A little smile flitted across her face.

"Us too?" Comfort murmured but Grandmother did not reply.

"Greetings, Bisi, greetings, Ya," she was saying to two women who had left their household tasks to come to the door of their compound. All Wanwangeri knew of Comfort's arrival the night before and, the children acting as outriders, everyone knew too of their approach. Did Kwame know she was coming, Comfort wondered.

"Greetings, Old One," Bisi replied smiling widely and tightening the single cloth wrapped round beneath her armpits which she wore at home. "So your been-to granddaughter has come back to you?"

"Onyame is good," Grandmother nodded reverently. The pride and affection in her smile was seasoned with triumph, Comfort noticed with alarm. She must not let Grandmother think she was staying for ever. Surely she didn't think it.

"Greetings, Comfort," Ya said smiling too while her eyes took in the too-short striped skirt wondering if it was the latest fashion. "It is good to have you back."

"Thank you, Ya," Comfort said. "It is good to be back but I'm only here for a month." Grandmother's hand on her shoulder tightened.

"Only a month?" Ya glanced from one to the other. "Such a long journey for such a short time?"

"I have to go back to school, my ticket is booked for September 3rd," Comfort tried to explain but Grandmother was already walking on, her stick hitting the ground sharply at every step. "Chu ... school ... cutting holes in people's heads ... such wickedness ..." she muttered as if to herself. The children, joined by others from all round the village, had grown to a horde, but wise to Grandmother's temper kept a safe distance. The sun was climbing high in the sky, lizards grey with orange throats, basked on the hot sand and scuttled out of the path as they approached. Dogs, spotted black or brown, wandered, scavenging for food.

"Greetings, old one, greetings, old mother, greetings, Comfort," the women called from the next compound. Most of the men in Wanwangeri were fishermen and had gone to the river long before. Only Tano, the carpenter, and Sika, the potter and headman, were still in the village at this time of day. Kwame, Comfort wondered, hearing the trundle of potting wheels turning and thinking of that afternoon, the fragile privacy of leaves! What would she do when she saw Kwame, where would she look?

"Greetings, old mother," Sika's voice came from the dimness of the large hut and the two hand-turned wheels trundled slowly down to stillness. "I have something for you." He got down from his high stool, wiping the clay from his hands, and handed her a postcard, the postcard Comfort had sent of the Ambassadors Hotel. "Greetings, Comfort, so you have come back to Wanwangeri?"

"Greetings, Sika," Comfort said looking down at her kickers. "But I'm only here for a month." It was a life-line, she had to say it. She glanced quickly into the hut where two small boys, temporarily freed from their wheelturning, gazed smiling and round-eyed in her direction.

"Greetings, Kwame," Grandmother said, peering into the darkness of the pottery and fanning herself with the postcard.

"Greetings, old one," Kwame said; his voice had deepened. He came to the door of the hut, grown to a young man, apprentice and heir to his father's trade, handsome, his skin shining and jet black, a curling fringe of lash above wide eyes. "Greetings,

Comfort. You can stay for longer surely?" He shook her hand, his own slightly tacky with clay.

"Greetings, Kwame," Comfort mumbled, hot and confused. She saw from his eyes that he certainly did remember that afternoon, and Grandmother's chuckle as she looked from one to the other, suggested she knew something of it too. It was hard to keep secrets in Wanwangeri. "I have to go back to school."

"School?" said Kwame wonderingly. "You still go to school?"

"Chu, school," said Grandmother scornfully. "School is for children and reading and writing. Tell her, Kwame, school is not for those whose womanhood has come to them."

"But I have to go back," Comfort muttered in a strangled voice, aware of the speculative gaze of their three pairs of eyes. It was her business wasn't it and nobody else's. Did Grandmother have to tell everybody? Was it such a big deal? But she knew from her previous visit that it would be futile to protest, worse than futile, because Grandmother had a mischievous streak and liked to tease. Grandmother would do and say what she wanted, she always had.

"'The eagle reared as a chicken will fly away'" Sika said, his eyes still resting on Comfort and liking what he saw. "Can this one cook?"

"'The crab does not produce a bird'," Grandmother said sharply. "She cooks well. She can prepare *garri* and *kenke* and *abomu* as well as any young woman in Wanwangeri." Did they have to talk about her as if she wasn't there? Comfort bit her lip angrily. You should always say what you thought, Margaret said, and do what you want.

Which was all very well. Grandmother walked on, her stick tip-tapping like a death watch beetle. When Comfort looked back over her shoulder, Sika and Kwame were still standing outside the pottery, talking together, heads close.

"Greetings, old one, greetings, Comfort, so you have come back?" they called from the next compound.

"Only for a month," Comfort said. She had to say it, it had to be said but the words came out louder than she meant and Grandmother's fingers digging at her shoulder were like iron claws. "I'm only stopping here for a month."

"Only for a month ... cutting holes in heads ... such foolishness ... such wickedness ..." Grandmother muttered swinging her stick scattering chickens and children as she turned for home. "When I was your age I learned from my grandmother's wisdom ... respect for custom ..."

"Did you see Kwame?" Tawia called as they entered the compound. She danced towards them with the fufu pole still clutched in her hand. "Every girl in Wanwangeri wants to be his calabash."

"Do not use that vulgar word," Grandmother hissed furiously. "'If a little bird talks like a big bird, it may hurt itself with the sound of its own voice.' Go back to your *fufu* and be quiet."

"Yes, Grandmother," Tawia said crestfallen. "Sorry, Grandmother."

"Come and help me chop vegetables, Comfort," Aunt Ata called. She was sitting in the shade of the roof which jutted out from the food store with her little son, Kwashi, quiet in the dust beside her.

"What?" Grandmother paused on her way to her hut, her eyes bright with anger. "Asking a visitor to work brings bad luck. In Ghana a visitor gets the best of everything and does not work."

"Wish I was a visitor," Tawia muttered as Grandmother disappeared into her hut and the coloured strip quivered and grew still. The children returned to the compound one by one and sensing Grandmother's mood, crept warily past.

"Shall I fetch water then?" Comfort said wanting to escape. "The drinking calabash is nearly empty."

"Tawia will fetch water," Grandmother's voice came distinctly from inside her hut.

"But ... but ... I want to work. I mean my granny lets me help, I always work in Penfold," Comfort said thinking for a moment of the strawberry fields. "A good quick picker." It would be plums by now and then early apples ...

"Only a month ... only a month ..." Grandmother muttered, "A visitor does not work in Wanwangeri, that is the custom."

Comfort cleared her throat. It was a contest of wills and she couldn't afford to lose. "I can only stay a month but I am not a visitor," she said in a voice which sounded stronger than she felt. "How can a granddaughter be a visitor? I'm fourteen and I have to go back to school but I belong to this family and this family belongs to me. 'The tree surrounded by the forest is not blown down by the hurricane'."

There was a pause and then Aunt Ata spoke. "Our daughter speaks well and knows our ways." She smiled reassuringly at Comfort. "Comfort is her father's child."

"Mante was always honey-tongued," Grandmother's voice mumbled more hurt than angry now. "But words are cheap."

"My father has many troubles ... and he has to work very hard ... and Efua ..."

"He has chosen his path," Grandmother said.

"And you have chosen yours," Comfort said astonished at her own boldness. Suddenly the Ga words, the old sayings were bright and fizzing on her tongue. "'The one cutting the path does not always see that the path is crooked'."

"Aye-aye ... Comfort speaks for true," Aunt Ata said and the deep laugh rumbled in her body as she handed her a chopping knife. "She flies in the air like a bird and as suddenly as a coconut drops from the tree, she comes to Wanwangeri, but she is part of the family. Comfort is not a visitor."

Inside her hut Grandmother was silent.

Comfort sat on her bed thinking of all that had happened and writing her diary. It was two days later. The strong smell of kerosene filling the hut was better, she supposed, than termites eating her bed. Perhaps she would get used to the smell. *Arrived at Wanwangeri*, she wrote for August 1st. *Saw Grandmother and talked a bit. Didn't see Kwame*, August 2nd. *Saw Kwame. Told Grandmother I was only staying a month. Grandmother very cross.*

It was all perfectly true but the pencilled words hardly expressed the complex and restless state of her feelings. A home of your own was the best thing in the world, Margaret said, and Comfort was the only girl at Lodge School with a house of her own even if it was only a mud hut. But she didn't find it all that wonderful. Her eyes considered the gritty red wall, not that she wasn't grateful and at least it was cool or cooler than outside anyway and it was nice to be able to get away from the children.

Grandmother's disappointment at the shortness of her stay had invaded Comfort's own feelings and made her disappointed with herself. But what could she do. For all the hut had been kept empty all this time, a gesture compelling in itself with a compound so crowded, and the bed made specially, the hut didn't seem more particularly her home than the attic bedroom at Smithy Cottage or the bed under the window of the dormitory at Lodge School.

What she really wanted was nothing to do with beds or huts but more to do with feelings. If Mante wanted her to stay that would be something else, she wanted Mante to love her, or like her at least, the way she was and Grandmother too. But people felt as they felt, Margaret said, and trying to change that was like banging your head against a brick wall. Comfort sighed, perhaps she was destined to be a head-banger all her life. She was born in the year of the rabbit, Maxine said, that's why she was as she was. More than anything she wanted to see Jeo.

Outside the worst heat of the day was over and the children gone out to play. The sewing machine whirred as Aunt Ata turned the handle, sewing Comfort's cloth, and Tawia pounded fufu for the evening meal, the endless rhythmical thud echoed in a dozen compounds beyond.

August 3rd. *Saw Kwame.* She narrowed her eyes, 'dreamseeing' green leaves, trying to fit the boy of two and a half years ago to the present young man. Had his eyes been as thick-fringed as they were now? All the girls in the village wanted to marry Kwame, Tawia said. Why else had Sika asked if she could cook unless he was looking for a wife for Kwame?

Suppose she was to marry Kwame, Comfort smiled to herself, exploring the notion in her mind like dipping a toe into the sea. One thing, she would be grown-up straight away. No more French or Latin or notices along the corridor or school reports or not talking after lights out, or holidays at Penfold. She would leave all that behind. Just for a moment the idea seemed intriguingly seductive. Kwame living in the clan house with his father and the other men and coming to her hut at night, the pottery business and Grandmother's cloth business and living in Wanwangeri for ever. But once chosen it would be the end of choice.

The other way was Lodge School and England and exams, and doing what you were told for years and years but after that … well you couldn't see after that because it wasn't mapped. Mante wanted her to be top of the form, didn't he. Well she would if she could. Five years … ten years … the future was an unknown place. The choices legion.

That night there was groundnut stew and *fufu*, Tawia's *fufu* made from yam pounded to a glutinous pulp, scooped up in hungry fingers but eaten delicately, even the small children cat-neat under Grandmother's watchful eye. Esi had returned from Akwapawa with news of a cloth sold that day and as soon as the meal was finished Grandmother wanted to hear not just the price obtained but the bargaining details, who said what and the dash. Esi, inspired by her audience, half-told, half-acted the story with much repartee and waving of hands. The children sat in a circle listening and enjoying the drama, learning the ways of the market and the customs of the Ga.

It was quite dark and the clear sky was speckled

with stars when the drumming began, drumming that tugged at the feet so even the small children already fallen asleep, woke and ran off with the others. Esi and Ata followed more slowly but however tired they felt the drums put the bounce back in their footsteps, Esi swaying in time to the rhythm as she walked, Ata turning in little circles. Even after a hard day's work nobody in Wanwangeri was too tired for dancing.

"And Comfort, are you going to dance?" Grandmother said.

"I think I would rather stay with you," said Comfort uncertainly. Ama had taught her to dance the handkerchief dance and the graceful *adowa* but could she remember all the steps. Besides Kwame would be watching, suppose he was to read her thoughts. And Kwame would be dancing too, his feet thudding on the hard earth. Men and women didn't dance together in Wanwangeri.

"You must learn the dances of the Ga, they are the spirit of our people. Esi will teach you and Ata," Grandmother said but she seemed glad of Comfort's presence that night nevertheless.

"Another time," Comfort said shyly. If she couldn't remember the precise steps she remembered how it was, how the drumming and dancing whirled faster and faster and caught you up like a merry-go-round and carried you away until you no longer knew who or what you were or what you wanted.

"I bought you this from England," Comfort said switching the small silvery torch off and on and feeling suddenly foolish. "I thought you might like it." But why should Grandmother like it just because she had liked it, a special switch turned the light red, green or white.

"Aye-aye, it is a fine-fine torch," Grandmother said smiling as her gnarled fingers switched it back and forth from red to green. "I shall keep it on my sleeping mat. An old women does not sleep well at night. Red and green and white will lighten the long dark night. Listen," Grandmother cupped her hand round her ear.

"What?" said Comfort turning her head towards the ball of light in the centre of Wanwangeri where pressure lamps hung from trees. She could hear Tete drumming and the thud of a hundred dancing feet and beyond that another sound, a single slow irregular beat coming from the west.

"Can you hear the talking drum?" Grandmother murmured.

"I hear it," Comfort said. "What does it say? Is there news of Efua and Jeo?"

"No news," Grandmother said. "It is telling a story." How could a drum tell a story, Comfort wondered and, as if she had heard the thought, Grandmother said proudly, "Reading the talking drums is an old skill, hard to learn, harder than reading books. My grandmother taught me. The drum has a thousand voices. It can croak like a frog or sing like a grasshopper or squeak like a bat. A good reader must learn them all."

"Could you teach me to read the talking drums?" Comfort whispered. The warm darkness made it a soft time, a confiding time.

"You need Ashanti blood to read them," Grandmother murmured.

"But you are Ga surely," Comfort said. "Mante says the Ga …"

"My son doesn't know everything," Grandmother

said with a little smile. "A mother keeps her secrets and a grandmother. That flying-in-the-air woman is not the only one with Ashanti blood. Long ago … a thousand thousand moons … the Ashanti and British were fighting, Kumasi was burnt down and Ashanti warriors ran into the bush and hid. Aye-aye, those were terrible times," Grandmother said rocking herself back and forth on her stool and staring into the darkness as if she were watching the past enacted. "My grandmother was a young woman then, very young, working alone in her farm. Suddenly a warrior jumped from the bushes where he had hidden … a very tall Ashanti wearing a leopard skin … she let him stay and gave him food. Later a daughter was born, my mother. Very tall she was and very fierce … fierce …" Grandmother's eyes had closed and her head slid forward so her chin rested on her chest. Comfort stared into the darkness seeing not the quiet compound and the circle of huts and the shadows thrown by the pressure lamp but a girl breaking the soil with her chungkol, a girl planting pawpaw seed and yam. The tall Ashanti warrior jumping from the bush, very tall and wearing a leopard skin … a golden necklet hung with golden bells and golden anklets hung with bells too which rang as he ran or jumped from the bushes.

"You are a quarter Ashanti then?" Comfort whispered and Grandmother mumbled in her sleep but did not wake.

Chapter 9

Comfort straightened her back and stood up to look at her handiwork. She had been in Wanwangeri for more than two weeks now and working on her farm for the greater part of the day. The green of cassava and yam was broken now by the patch or dark red earth where she had broken the soil with a borrowed chungkol, ready for sowing. Tomorrow she would plant the seeds, tomato and green beans and hot peppers which Esi had given her. Her back ached with the unaccustomed crouching and her hands were sore. Bisi and Ya had been working together on their farms earlier and the three of them had chatted, and Tawia had brought her water to drink, but for most of the day, Comfort had been alone.

The farm was just outside the village and between trunks of palm trees, straight and grey as pencils, she could see the ragged compound fences and pyramids of thatched huts rising above them. Now the sun was beginning to slide towards the horizon, blue smoke rising in a dozen separate threads against the pink sky meant cooking had begun for the evening meal.

Comfort spat on her blistered hands wiping the earth away with a rag and took out her diary. It was difficult to get it written when she was never alone except at night when the hut was dark. Two yellow-green pawpaw cut from her tree, lay at her feet ready to be carried back to Grandmother especially fond of the pink sweet-sour flesh.

With the evening a slight breeze stirred the bushes round, fluttering leaves. Comfort gazed round apprehensively. Under the bushes there was deep purple shade. What of the Ashanti warrior who had hidden all those years ago clad in leopard skin and golden bells. Where had he hidden? Her great-great-grandmother, where had she found him? Had she been breaking the earth on this very same farm? It was family land, theirs and Onyame's.

August 8th. *I am one-sixteenth Ashanti*, Comfort wrote, *and seven-sixteenths Ga and eight-sixteenths English.* That Ashanti warrior was her great-great-grandfather. Her roots. And one of her great-great-great grandmothers had been an Ashanti woman. Her bones lay somewhere in Ashanti land. At Kumasi, the capital perhaps, or even at Krempepong. She, Comfort, might well be related to Efua, her step-mother. Was that why she wanted to see little Jeo so very much. *Jeo is nine-sixteenths Ashanti*, she wrote, *and only seven-sixteenths Ga.*

Half-caste they called her innocently enough at Lodge School and Comfort smiled and said nothing. She was used to such words, mulatto, wog, mongrel they had said at the London schools, sometimes teasing sometimes not. She had to get used to teasing, Margaret said, which was all very well. But who was pure-bred pedigree anyway, only royalty and horses and dogs. If English people were a mixture of Celtic and Roman and Anglo-Saxon they were mongrels too, the difference was they were white.

A stick cracked. Footfalls. Comfort jumped up, startled, but the person who came along the path in a faded blue and yellow cloth was no Ashanti warrior but Ama, her cousin.

"Akwaba, Ama, greetings. Oh, it's great to see you," Comfort cried. The two girls ran together and flung their arms round each other's necks.

"Greetings, Comfort," Ama said speaking in the English she hardly ever used now. "I walk from Preko's village, I cannot come before." It was only then that Comfort noticed the child, Kofi, sleeping on Ama's back but waking now as the two sat down on a fallen palm trunk and Ama untied her cloth.

"I wondered if you would come," Comfort said.

"Of course I am coming to see my sister," Ama said smiling and taking Kofi onto her lap. "And Kofi want to see you, too, eh, Kofi?" Comfort smiled and put out her hand but the little boy turned his head shyly away.

"He's a fine boy," she said politely, no less was expected. Ama sighed, letting him slide to the ground where he clung to her knees, his thumb in his mouth. The scald was immediately visible, livid and white on his leg, a line in the centre all pink and puckered like a zip fastener.

"Poor little boy, it must have been awful," Comfort said and Ama's eyes filled with ready tears. "But surely it's over now, his leg is better ... almost."

"It is never over for me," Ama said miserably. "Always the leg is there to see and shame me." Her face was still the face of a fifteen year old but too thin now, the skin tightly drawn across her cheeks, and in her expression as she looked at Kofi pity mingled with dislike. "He pull boiling saucepan but they say it is my fault, Preko and Preko's mother, all his family are blaming me, Grandmother too." Suddenly she pulled the little boy back into her lap and buried her face against his crisp hair, and wept.

"Sorry ..." Comfort whispered saddened by Ama's grief but not knowing what to say. "Sorry ..."

"Oh, Comfort, oh ... I didn't mean ..." Ama blew her nose onto the ground and wiped her face on the edge of her cloth and set the boy onto the ground once more.

"Go ... play ..." she instructed waving her hand but the child stood where he was, holding her cloth, used to being the centre of everyone's concern. His scalded leg was thinner than the other and somewhat wasted. As Ama said, what had happened would never be forgotten. He stared from one to the other with dark accusing eyes.

"Well, tell me about everything ... everything that has happened since I left," Comfort said trying to recapture lost days. The two of them had been such friends when Comfort stayed before. Then Ama, only a year older but Ghanaian born and expert on all matters in Wanwangeri, had been her guide and adviser. They had shared a hut, lying on their sleeping mats side by side and talking far into the night in the carefree days before Ama's ceremony.

"What's there to tell?" Ama shrugged sadly.

"Mante told me you were married," Comfort said thinking of the letter. How she had lain in bed that night with the letter under her pillow, listening to the quiet breathing in the dormitory round her and the grey Folkestone sea breaking on the beach. She had thought of Ama and Preko then, close together and happy. Grandmother would be pleased. How easy it was for Ama to please Grandmother but how difficult for Comfort. Grandmother wanting her to be her eyes and ears, wanting it still, wanting her to be business-clever and cloth-clever, Granny wanting prefect and good school reports, it was impossible to please them both. A good education was important for a girl, Granny said, especially a girl like Comfort.

"Aye-aye," Ama smiled wanly, not wanting to talk about her marriage and all that had followed. "Do you remember my ceremony?" she said. "Ten children scrambling after a bit of egg." They both laughed, it had meant Ama was going to bear ten children. The prospect had delighted her then but did little to revive her spirits now. "You give me red handbag."

"Yes," Comfort said.

"Grandmother, she is often talking of you," Ama said glancing sideways. "She show me postcards. Mante's Comfort is her favourite, they are saying, 'Only palm fruit doesn't get lost in the fire'." She swept Kofi's pebbles from her lap with a sudden angry gesture. "Grandmother always say you coming back one day."

"But I am only here for a month," Comfort said.

That night there was palm soup, palm nuts boiled and pounded, oily and tangerine red, and fish freshly caught in the river by Ata's husband, Obodai, and boiled rice.

"I take my father his food tonight," Ama said switching to Ga as they entered the compound, carrying the bowls of hot food to the men's compound with Tawia. Kofi released from his mother's cloth, staggered to Grandmother's outstretched arms, and Grandmother scooped him onto her lap, examining his hurt leg with little clucks of dismay, cuddling him close in a way she never did with other children in the compound. Was it because of his hurt, Comfort wondered, or because he was her first great grandchild. There was indeed something very touching about the little boy with his big sad eyes. A baby of your own was the best thing there was, Margaret said, but had she meant at fifteen. When Ama returned she took the boy, spooning palm soup into her own mouth and trying to spoon it into his, and when he turned his head away, offering her breast instead. Her dark unhappy eyes circled the faces round waiting for criticism. Too much had gone wrong in Ama's short life.

"Comfort's cloth is sewn," Ata said after the meal was finished.

"Brilliant," Comfort said retiring to her hut and putting on the blouse and lower cloth, smoothing the cotton, yellow sunflowers on dark red, the power of life, emerging self-consciously.

"Aye-aye ... my fine been-to granddaughter in her fine-fine cloth," Grandmother cackled.

"Fine-fine cloth," the children echoed nodding and everybody clapped.

"Now when the drumming starts my granddaughter can dance," Grandmother said. "Now she can go to the market at Akwapawa." Comfort opened her mouth in surprise and then shut it again. She had only been allowed to go to the market after weeks of patient negotiation last

122

time but words were better left unsaid when Grandmother could so easily change her mind.

"Thank you, Grandmother, thank you, Ata, for sewing it," Comfort said politely and seeing a glance exchanged between Ata and Esi was suddenly aware of Ama's envious gaze and shabby cloth as she suckled Kofi.

"'The chicken which is nearest the mother eats the thigh of the grasshopper'," Ata's usual friendliness was tinged with resentment.

"Well … well … perhaps Ama could have a new cloth too?" Comfort burst out. "It's only fair."

"Who speaks of fair? Must I give cloth as well as many cedis to Preko's family?" Grandmother's eyes flashed angrily. "When Preko is pleased with his wife he will give her new cloth …"

"It wasn't my fault." Ama pulled Kofi abruptly from her breast and pulled down her blouse. Her expression was resentful.

"No mother can watch her child every minute," Esi said soothingly.

"You speak for true," Grandmother said with a sage and more conciliatory air. "Ama is a good babyful wife to Preko … not a flying-in-the-air woman or a cutting-hole-in-head woman. Soon there will be other children and Preko's family will forgive."

That night Ama lay down on the sleeping mat in Comfort's hut where Kofi was already asleep. "It's like the old days," she whispered. "Do you remember how we used to talk and talk? Aye-aye, everything is changed now. I wish you would stay."

"I can't," Comfort said gazing at the doorway, the strips stirred a little in the night wind, black against the great white eye of the almost full moon.

123

"Do you like Kwame, you used to?" Ama giggled a little. "Him and his leafy tree, every girl in Wanwangeri climb into Kwame's tree."

"Even you?" Comfort whispered.

"Even me," Ama agreed and added primly. "Long time before Preko of course. They say Sika come to visit Grandmother soon," she added slyly but when Comfort didn't answer she turned on her side, and cocooning herself and Kofi in the faded cloth, she fell asleep.

In the morning Ama ate a bowl of cold rice, tied Kofi to her cloth and set off for her own village. Comfort walked to the edge of Wanwangeri and stood in the path waving until Ama disappeared round the bend in the sandy path.

The air was still and cool and Comfort breathed deeply, listening to the sounds of Wanwangeri, monkeys chittering in the trees above, and the squawk and trill of birds, the shouts of fishermen as canoes were launched into the river. She had been pleased to see Ama but was not sorry to see her go.

Ten minutes later she rolled the sleeping mat and swept the floor with a handful of twigs tied at the top. Bob Geldof stared impassive from the wall. *Ama left today*, Comfort wrote on August 19th. *Kofi has an awful scar. Poor Kofi.* Preko was angry still, Ama said. How long would he be angry? Poor Ama. *Saw Kwame.* Dark eyes shining and a thick curl of lash. Green leaves, deep green shadows. Her heart was pounding still. *Kwame says we must talk.*

Chapter 10

Early next day Comfort set off to the market at Akwapawa with Ata. They carried the new cloth on their heads, divided between them just as it had been on the journey from Accra but now Comfort was wearing one of the cloths. Leaves wet with dew brushed at her hands each side of the track and a little way away where the trees were closer, wraiths of white mist hovered between the trunks. The track meandered and soon Wanwangeri was out of sight. Grandmother had been not merely willing but eager for her to go to the market, Comfort thought. It was curious that. Was it because she knew she enjoyed it and was market-clever, or was it something more subtle, a way of inducing her to stay altogether, to give up her 'only for a month'. There was often a shrewd gleam in Grandmother's eagle-bright eyes.

Still it was brilliant to be going to Akwapawa. In Wanwangeri time moved at a slow pace and every day was the same. Right now Grandmother would be sitting on her stool dozing in the sun as usual and waking intermittently to scold a wayward child. Esi and Tawia would be washing pots and whitening the hearth like women all round the village. As for Kwame, he would be carrying the finished pots to dry on the shelf ready for firing. When would they talk and what would Kwame say, what would she?

In Akwapawa there was so much happening, lorries and traders coming and going, constant bustle and change. She would find the market was somewhat different, Aunt Ata had explained. The Hausa man who had brought cloth from Kumasi for as long as anyone could remember, a gentle cunning old man driving a bargain without hurry in the customary way, had finally died and his business passed to a nephew, Abdul. Abdul cared nothing for the customary ways but only for profit, the quicker the better. 'Time is money.' He had put up the price of his cloth so much that the market women would and could no longer buy from him, a struggle of wills. A few like Ata had the money and know-how to travel to Accra and buy for themselves but the smaller traders had neither resource and their trade was suffering. Comfort frowned as she followed the dusty track, trying to remember all Mante has said about self-reliance and house cleaning and green pineapples for export. Had he said anything about markets?

The sun was high by the time they reached Akwapawa and the tarmaced main street and surface of the lorry park gleamed dazzling white like snow. Ata blinked and walked straight under the shade of the market roof but Comfort paused a moment, suddenly shy, less concerned with changes in the market and more concerned whether the market women would remember her.

She looked round for Grandmother's lorry, *Dry Leaf Fall*, to prolong the moment. The driver and the bookman had gone to the coffee house and she stood by the green bonnet tracing the motto with her finger and remembering. She had been shy last time and little Bolo, lying under the stall, had been such a help on her first day. "'Both the green leaf and the dry leaf fall'," Grandmother had murmured when Bolo died. Comfort had copied the saying into the back of an exercise book at Lodge School. Bolo, the green leaf, had fallen already and it was hard to accept that Grandmother, strong-willed and indomitable as she seemed, would one day die, that the dry leaf would fall.

Comfort sighed and took a deep breath and went into the market after Ata. Tall metal piers supported the corrugated iron roof and were painted in peeling dark green. There were hundreds of baskets and the floor was littered with scraps of vegetable, squashed tomatoes and decaying cabbage leaves. All round traders, women and children mostly, were opening up stalls and spreading out their wares. Shouts and chatter, snatches of laughter echoed and reverberated in the high roof like a drum and white teeth flashed in the shadowed light. The market belonged to women. The market mammies who came each day with their babies on their backs and their goods on their heads, established a second home behind their stalls where food was often eaten, children played and gossip was exchanged as well as business.

"Aye-aye, it's Comfort, isn't it?" Abla called from the next stall, embracing Comfort and laughing richly. "Aye-aye, been-to Comfort has come back to us," she teased. Comfort laughed too then, laughed with relief and joy, breathing Abla's violet-scented talcum and feeling her hand touch something soft and damp, the new baby on Abla's back, recently outdoored and pale-skinned still.

"Another boy, Adee," Abla said proudly.

But when Comfort and Ata laid the new cloth in a daisy circle on the stall a few moments later Comfort's uneasiness returned. Abla had been friendly but now she was aware of the word going round, eyes turning to gaze in her direction, voices murmuring, "Aye-aye, it's Comfort, old Comfort's been-to granddaughter." But smiles were bleak and greetings low-key. Something was wrong, but what. Somehow she had offended them.

When Ata went to talk to the driver of *Dry Leaf Fall*, Comfort was alone at the stall. It was still early for customers but several market mammies were gazing in her direction and their eyes were cool rather than friendly. Comfort swallowed, had they forgotten their clown and darling, how they had laughed at her inventive and lively calls. What of the formidable Ghanaian heart? Her sojourn at the market previously had been heady with excitement and she longed to find her bubbling, outgoing market self again, her Ghanaian self. She had been different then, eleven years old and clear as a bell and ready for anything, walking a knife-edge everyday between acceptable humour and outrageous cheek. But she was fourteen now.

A sudden stinging slap on her arm startled Comfort, "What you doing, white girl?" a woman shouted, gaunt and wild-eyed. "What for you come to market? White girl not fit for market."

"But I'm ... I'm Comfort Kwatey-Jones ... I'm not white ..." Comfort gasped out, jumping up.

"Leave her, Manko," shouted Abla from the next stall.

"Go away, go away, go away," the woman shrieked like an owl, slapping with each shriek.

"Stop that, Manko," Aunt Ata shouted hurrying back and tightening her cloth ready for action. "What for you slap my daughter? What for, eh?"

"What for you bring white girl to market?" Manko shouted turning away. "This girl not fit for this place ..."

"Are you all right? That one sky-sky," Aunt Ata tapped her head significantly.

"What did she mean white girl? What did she want?" Comfort's voice quavered and she dropped abruptly onto the wooden box behind the stall, unnerved rather than hurt by the sudden assault, her knees were shaking and tears pricked the back of her eyes. Half-white and half-black was black in England but white in Ghana it seemed. The market had never been like this.

"Pay her no heed," Ata said. "Manko's a poor thing, her stock is small and her business is failing."

"Do not mind her," one or two others called out sympathetically nodding and waving, more friendly now which was something at least. And now Comfort looked more closely she saw that though vegetables were plentiful, the cloth displays laid out were meagre and shabby and the cloth mammies themselves were shabby too. Once they had modelled their latest, most fashionable cloths on their own persons but now there was a flacidity about their shoulders, a dispirited air, and many had lost weight. Times were hard in Akwapawa market.

"Come and buy my cloth," Ata began to call to passersby. "Good cloth, latest fashion, very cheap price, lady. You want to look?"

"Come and buy my cloth," Comfort echoed, copying Ata's tone, though her voice was small and a little husky. "Very good cloth from Accra."

Eyes swivelled in her direction and at once smiling faces straightened again into an alarming coldness. What was wrong, Comfort wondered. What not-done thing was she doing. Everywhere there were different not done things. Once she had known. Once she had been street-wise and market-wise but after two years at Lodge School she was French-wise and netball-wise and exam-wise but street-wise no longer and her courage faltered. Customers had begun to stop at the stall fingering the different cloths laid out and now the gaze of the market mammies was definitely hostile.

"New-fangled cloth straight from Accra," Comfort choked. "Be Miss Akwapawa, Beauty Queen, in this fine fine cloth." Nobody smiled.

"Hush up about Accra," Ata said. "I can afford the journey but most of the mammies cannot and they do not like to be reminded."

"Sorry ... sorry," Comfort said abashed and silenced by her lack of tact. She ought to have realised. "It's a shame," she added a moment later. "Couldn't Grandmother send *Dry Leaf Fall* to Kumasi to get cloth for everybody?"

"You ask her," Ata said rolling her eyes expressively. "I try and try a hundred times. She listens to you. 'The chicken nearest to mother eats the thigh of the grasshopper'," she finished and there was no resentment in her tone this time.

Comfort might have privileges not accorded to

the other grandchildren but she also had extra difficulties.

"Can you take Adee for a while?" Abla said a few moments later. "Hausa man's nephew is in the coffee shop and some of us are going to talk to him."

"Good luck then," Comfort said as she tied the small baby onto her back. She had often carried babies for women in the market but never one as small as Adee before. She had never felt so tenderly before either, a soft melting in her mouth and belly as she twisted her neck to see his little head nestling against her shoulder. Jeo had been six months old and much bigger by the time she saw him. When would there be news of Jeo?

"Buy my cloth, lady, very nice cloth, very cheap price," Ata called to a passing woman.

"Hush," whispered Comfort as Adee stirred restlessly against her back. "He is not used to market noises yet."

"What did Abdul say?" Ata asked as the market women returned from the coffee shop, forlorn and silent.

"Nothing good," Abla said. "'How can we buy at such prices?' we say but he smiles and smiles and does not listen. 'Business is business, put up your prices too', he says, 'let the people of Akwapawa pay more'."

"But surely," Comfort said, untying her cloth reluctantly and passing the sleeping Adee back to his mother. "If the market women can't buy his cloth he will lose his business?"

"Aye-aye, we tell him this but he sells cloth to many villages besides Akwapawa," Abla said. "He thinks he can force us to buy at this price."

"'The young eagle wants to try the strength of his wings'," Ata added.

Comfort wandered away across the lorry park. *Dry Leaf Fall* had left on its journey and she crossed the main road and wandered slowly past the coffee shop. There were no women there but a Syrian and several Hausa men sat drinking coffee and talking in low voices. Which one was the Hausa man's nephew, Abdul, Comfort wondered. Angry words rehearsed themselves in her head and struggled towards her throat. A Hausa man was looking in her direction, his small eyes squinted shrewdly and he muttered something to his neighbour. There was a low laugh all round the coffee shop and a licking of lips and her angry words shrivelled and flaked to nothing like burnt paper and Comfort turned away.

"And what did my granddaughter sell today?" Grandmother asked when they returned that evening. Esi was pounding fufu and Tawia stirring the stew pot for the evening meal. It was just beginning to get dark and the air was flavoured with blue smoke and spice as cooking began. The children sat watching hungrily and waiting.

"Comfort did well," Ata said picking up her little son, Kwashi. "She called in a voice like a baby finch just hatched but she sold the blue cloth patterned with peacock feathers for a good price."

"Aye-aye, she is truly the child of this family," Grandmother said, her head resting on her stick. "A been-to girl but market-clever just as I was. What did she shout?" Grandmother's eyes circled towards Comfort seeking entertainment. Too old to go to the market herself she liked to re-live her market time, the best years of her life, with a full and lively account of all that was happening at Akwapawa every day.

"Nothing much, Grandmother," Comfort said flatly. She was thinking about the market women, she must do something if she could. She was thinking about Jeo too. "What of the talking drums of Krempepong, did they speak today?"

"If they spoke I did not hear them," Grandmother said determined to have her way. "Did you see Abla today? Tell me about the market."

"Nothing," Comfort muttered.

"Nothing?" Grandmother's eyes rounded. "How nothing?"

"Manko slapped Comfort," Ata put quickly.

"She is sky-sky, that one," Grandmother said. "Sorry sorry."

"Sky-sky," the children chorussed. "Sorry-sorry."

"Do not heed Manko, she is small woman and her business is failing, they say. Tell me what you called in the market, Comfort," Grandmother persisted. "Let me hear your words."

"Comfort called well," Ata said diplomatically. "Buy my cloth and be the Beauty Queen of Akwapawa, what else, Comfort?"

"Buy my cloth and be bright as a pineapple," Comfort muttered still oppressed by the plight of the market woman. "Buy my cloth and be pretty as a glossy starling."

Grandmother chuckled appreciatively, "Pretty as a glossy starling ... I like that."

"But the market's not a good place any more," Comfort burst out. "The Hausa man's nephew has put up his prices and nobody can buy."

"Chu," said Grandmother. "Times are bad. Let

them go to Accra for cloth, let them send their daughters as I must do."

"They cannot afford to," Ata said. "Women and children must eat. Food is expensive and prices rise all the time. One time they doubled overnight."

"What have such things to do with an old woman like me?" Grandmother said angrily. "Can I help it if prices rise?"

"You could let *Dry Leaf Fall* go to Kumasi to buy cloth," Comfort said. What did it matter if people got angry, Margaret said.

There was a moment's pause. Grandmother stared at Comfort in surprise and then began to rock back and forth on her stool in time to her lamentation. "Am I to be discarded like an old sponge? Aye-aye … my granddaughter is trying to ruin my lorry business. My customers wait and wait for *Dry Leaf Fall* but when it does not come they take *Fear Women* or *Beggar Has No Choice*. What am I to do? Aye-aye, my book-clever granddaughter is not lorry clever."

Comfort's hand flew to the ring at her neck and she took a deep breath. Words were only words, not sticks and stones, Margaret said. "I could be lorry-clever and market-clever too if you let me. *Dry Leaf Fall* doesn't run on Sunday anyway, does it, so why not let it go to Kumasi for cloth on Sunday?"

There was another pause. Nobody in the compound spoke to Grandmother like that. Nobody ever had. She stopped rocking and stared at Comfort with narrowed eyes.

"'The child cracks the shell of the snail but not that of the tortoise'," she croaked hoarsely.

"But I am not a child, Grandmother," Comfort said.

"Only a child is allowed such ignorance," Grandmother said. "*Dry Leaf Fall* must be cleaned, a dirty lorry is not good for business. Every Sunday *Dry Leaf Fall* must be cleaned."

"But Kumasi isn't far," Comfort said, keeping her voice steady. "*Dry Leaf Fall* can go in the morning and be washed in the afternoon."

"Aye-aye ... my only-a-month granddaughter wants to run my lorry business," Grandmother moaned. "Oh, it was a sad day ... a sad day when the letter came. My son marrying a white woman and a child expected already, a white child. Aye-aye ... my only son ... rue the day. What did we know of the woman's health and cooking ... the respectability of her family? ... What does a foolish young man know of such things?"

"Well ... I think Granny and Grandad Barton are respectable," Comfort said carefully. "Well ... very respectable really ... and healthy too. Margaret could cook quite well ... only she didn't like it much ... I used to do most of the cooking ..." Her voice trailed off.

"An English grandchild," Grandmother moaned dismally. " 'The crab does not produce a bird' ..." Her voice rose to a shriek and her stick struck the ground, scattering chickens and brown feathers. "Get out of my sight."

"Hush, now hush," Ata said soothingly, her arm round her mother's shoulders. "You speak with too much anger. It is not good for you. Are you not rich in grand-children?"

"Onyame be praised," Grandmother said.

"Take these to the men's house," Esi said thrusting bowls of hot food into the hands of Comfort and Tawia. "Quick."

"You make our grandmother angry when you argue so," Tawia murmured into the darkness between the compounds, her voice was both reproachful and admiring.

"I can't help it," Comfort said. "*Dry Leaf Fall* could go to Kumasi. Grandmother's not always right."

"But it does not do to say so," Tawia murmured primly as they entered the men's compound. Several men were sitting on stools in front of their huts, newly bathed after work and waiting for their hot meals.

"Father, I bring you food," Tawia said politely.

"Ah, Tawia, thank you, daughter," her father said.

"Greetings, Comfort," Obodai, Ata's husband, looked appraisingly at her new red cloth. "Aye-aye ... you have adopted the Ghanaian way of dressing and come back to us a grown woman? Are you looking for a husband here perhaps?"

The men chuckled appreciatively, glancing in Comfort's direction.

"No thanks," she mumbled, hot and embarrassed by their gaze, acutely aware that Kwame had just come into the compound carrying his father's stool. His eyes under the wooden curve watched her. "Not yet."

"Not yet?" Obodai repeated teasingly. "But we have plump and handsome young men living here. What do you want? The fine-fine son of headman or perhaps you are waiting for the son of a chief?" There was a ripple of teasing laughter all round.

"No ... yes ... I mean ... I'm only here for a month," Comfort said. She thrust the bowl of food unceremoniously into Obodai's hands and walked out of the compound with her head held high. Her heart was thudding unpleasantly as she waited for Tawia. Why couldn't they leave her alone?

"Pay them no heed," Tawia said shrugging her small shoulders airily. "They say things like that to me all the time, you know, but I do not mind. Chicken soup, they call me, a too-young girl is chicken soup."

"Why don't they come and fetch their own food?" Comfort said crossly. "We've both been working all day. Are they cripples or what?"

"Do not speak of such things," Tawia whispered in a shocked voice. "It is very bad luck. Besides how can men eat in a compound where there is chatter and children and pots to be washed and they have serious things to be discussed? Oh, I do like Kwame so," she added sadly. "He likes me but it's too long to wait."

Back in the Grandmother's compound the evening meal had already started. It was bad manners to talk while eating anyway and with Grandmother in a bad mood the children sat huddled and subdued. As soon as she had finished washing the bowls and pots Comfort retreated to her own hut, sitting just behind the ribboned doorway gazing up at the black sky and breathing in the velvety darkness. Your own house was the best thing in the world, Margaret said. But that night her own hut did not console her. Nothing was good when Grandmother was angry. Soon the compound was quiet and the village outside seemed unnaturally quiet too, as if all Wanwangeri grieved when Grandmother was angry.

And then Comfort heard it, a faint drumming so far away, the talking drums, the complicated rhythms she couldn't understand. And then the drumming was louder because the village next to Wanwangeri had heard the message and was passing it on. Comfort sat up straight and tense in the darkness. Her ears burned with the strain of listening. Her skin felt stretched as the skin of a drum itself and still the drumming went on. And now Tete was starting to drum, a drumming which throbbed right through her head, right through her whole body. Comfort ran out.

"Aye-aye, Onyame is to be praised," Grandmother stood outside her hut, her arms and stick raised towards the starry sky and Esi and Ata stood beside her and the children slid from their huts one by one, faces shining with expectation.

"The child is born in Krempepong, Efua has given us a fine boy this day ... the talking drum has told us," Grandmother cried in a high-pitched voice that was almost a wail. "My son Mante has a second son, Onyame be praised."

"Onyame be praised," Comfort chorussed with the others. She dropped on the stool close to Grandmother, took hold of her hand and whispered, "Is there news of Jeo?"

But there was tumult all round her now, the talking drums finished, the dancing drums began and already Ata and Esi and the children were pouring out of the compound towards the centre of the village. Grandmother went, too, leaning heavily on Ata's shoulder, her stick and her feet seemed to move in time to the drumming as Wanwangeri gathered in the centre of the village to dance all night.

Chapter 11

August 25th. *Dry Leaf is Going to Kumasi next Sunday for cloth,* Comfort wrote smiling to herself, sitting at the stall in the stifling midday heat while the Akwapawa market dozed round her. The atmosphere of the market was better now. Ata stretched out under the stall, slept with a little hissing snore. Abla and her three children shared one mat. But Comfort could not get used to such public sleeping. *But Grandmother won't let me go.* Comfort sighed, she would like to have seen Kumasi. Hadn't her ancestors come from Kumasi, she 'dream-saw' the burning town, could dream-see to the great blue lake at Krempepong not far away. She nibbled her pencil thoughtfully. What had made Grandmother change her mind in the first place, she who was famous for her obstinacy? Had she been convinced by Comfort's arguments or was it just her joy at the birth of Efua's baby? Whichever it was the message of the talking drums had sweetened her out of her usual complaints and scoldings. For two days she had sat in the shaded

139

doorway of her hut receiving all who came to offer felicitations with benign smiles.

"Onyame is good," she said over and over. "Aye-aye ... I am a poor woman but rich in grandchildren."

"You are lucky in your family. 'The trees surrounded by forest withstands the hurricane when the lone tree is blown down'," the visitors replied politely. Some of them owed her money and nobody wanted to spoil the occasion by reminding her that she was the richest woman in Wanwangeri with her cloth business and lorry business and much land besides. More still by the cocoa harvest, when Joshua, unable to re-pay his loan, would forfeit his farm to her, but who thought of such things on such a happy day. "You are indeed rich in grand-children. How many is it now?"

"Who can say?" Grandmother murmured, unwilling to commit herself to a precise figure and attract the envy and ill-wishing of less fortunate women and perhaps the wrath of the Gods. Comfort, sweeping the compound and not bound by any such anxieties, had counted on her fingers. Mante had three children now, Esi had six and Ata seven, so Grandmother had sixteen grand-children, not counting the five who had returned to their sky-family. Granny at Penfold had only one.

The new baby changed Grandmother's habits in other ways too. She no longer complained about Mante's disrespect for custom but instead talked nostalgically of his childhood, with Comfort sitting on the stool beside her. The gift, her only son, who had come to her so late in life, the bright little boy whose laugh trilled like a dawn chorus which lasted all day. The long journey to the mission school where she left him when he was five, knowing such education would turn her chick into a soaring eagle. The tears which had poured down his face like the rivers of the Black and White Voltas after rain. She had not dared look back and had not seen him again for more than a year. By then the boy, Mante, had changed, taller and thinner, he laughed less often and it was a different laugh, wary and constrained. As she listened Comfort saw the face of the weeping five year old as clearly as she saw the photograph of Mante in her hand.

It was several days since she had written her diary and there were back pages to fill in. *Stayed at home all day*, she wrote for August 22nd, wondering as she wrote was the hut in Wanwangeri really home. It was certainly home for a myriad insects which flicked and ticked in the shadowy thatch. She had lain on her bed in the heat of the day and watched as a column of ants advanced through the doorway and across the floor in a thick black line and then suddenly she jumped up, scuffling them back towards the doorway with the soles of her feet, finishing the job with the bundle of twigs kept for sweeping, throwing the disciplined line into disorganised panic. It was like a war, Comfort thought, the Ashanti fleeing from the British forces, the red of her cloth was the colour of war. Fighting and conquest was the old world, Mante said, now subjugation of poor natives was achieved by the withholding of loans, starvation perhaps but not bloodshed.

For several days Grandmother had wanted her to stay at Wanwangeri and Comfort had been happy enough to comply, fetching water, pounding fufu, preparing and cooking food, and above all listening. The market had been brilliant and Comfort market-clever, everyone said so, selling plenty of cloth at the fixed price and getting a good dash as well, but it was her easy acceptance by the market women which made it brilliant. She had run all over the market then, minding stalls and babies and writing letters for those who couldn't write, allowed a license and freedom by them certainly not allowed to their own daughters; Mante's been-to child, old Comfort's grandchild. But now it was different, trade was bad and the market women disgruntled and upset by Abdul's rise in prices, and nothing came her way but sour looks. It wasn't fair, Comfort thought, but nobody but a four-year-old child expected life to be fair, according to Granny at Penfold.

Saw Kwame. Went to Joshua's farm, August 24th, Comfort wrote. *Awful-awful.* It had been quite a long way to Joshua's farm but Grandmother had insisted that they walk as far one afternoon. No sound but the tap-tap of her stick and the squawk of startled birds as they left the village. Cocoa trees on either side of the path, growing twice the height of a man and planted in lines, large dark green leaves and great nuts large as marrows near the top.

"Fine-fine nuts," Grandmother murmured pausing to rest and breathe deeply for a moment. "Soon they will be ripe. Look, that one is yellow at the top already."

Comfort looked obediently but the instruction, the eager light in Grandmother's eyes made her uneasy. Beyond she could see Joshua's derelict hut.

"Cocoa harvest is the best time of year," Grandmother remarked as they walked on.

"Everyone working together, the whole village helping and such feasting … aye-aye … such dancing. Perhaps you will help with the harvest this year, Comfort?"

"But …" Comfort began to explain. She knew what to say, cocoa harvest was a month away and by then she would be back at school, but somehow the words flew out of her head like birds. "But …"

Joshua had come out of his hut to greet them, his chin stubbly and his manner obsequious, but a smell of palm wine and misery hung about him. He shouted over his shoulder to two thin and pot-bellied children who disappeared behind the hut.

"Sit down, sit down," he invited pushing a dusty stool towards them. "Bring cold drink for old Comfort, our benefactor," he shouted.

"And what of the harvest?" Grandmother inquired, peering round with an air which seemed to Comfort distinctly proprietory.

"Aye-aye, harvest will be good," Joshua said and his hand rubbed across his stubbled face with a rasping sound. "But prices are low and if everybody has a good harvest they go lower still."

"One crop is precarious, that is what the government tells us," Grandmother said. "You should grow other crops as well."

"Perhaps …" Joshua stared at the ground, unable either to argue or to meet the critical intensity of Grandmother's gaze. "If you give me more time …"

"Time is something I cannot give you. 'To lose an elephant for wren is foolish.' I am an old woman and have not enough time myself." Her lips were moving as she turned back to the path.

"Comfort … speak for me …" Joshua pleaded as Comfort hurried after her.

143

For a little way they walked in silence through the cocoa trees. What could she say, Comfort wondered, walking slowly, keeping her feet in time to Grandmother's stick. She knew without looking that Joshua was still standing on the path watching them but whatever she said it would only make things worse.

"It is good land this," Grandmother remarked, pausing a moment to poke a patch of loose soil with her stick. "Joshua owes me seven hundred cedis ... and after the harvest ... it belongs to me. Onyame is good."

"But why ..." Comfort began as they walked on. "I mean ... I mean ..." They were passing the place of Kwame's tree, was it this tree or the next Comfort wondered, momentarily abandoning the problem of Joshua.

"Last year I lend Joshua five hundred cedis when the harvest is bad," Grandmother explained. "But Joshua, he never pays me even the interest he owes ... and now he owes seven hundred and fifty cedis and cannot pay."

"Two hundred and fifty cedis is very high interest surely?" Comfort said.

"Fifty per cent. High risk too," Grandmother snapped but there was an uneasiness about her eyes. Sika, the headman had disapproved of the loan, others in Wanwangeri, too, though a high rate of interest for land was usual. "'If you want to eat toad look for a juicy one first'." Grandmother finished and her lips twitched into a smile both shrewd and guilty.

"But perhaps if you give Joshua another year ..." Comfort said. "I mean where will he go ... and his wife ... if you take his land?"

"Chu," Grandmother snorted derisively. "He is a small-small man and a big-big drinker and his family must take care of him."

It was early evening by the time they got back to the village. Men and women were coming up from the river with baskets full of fish on their heads.

"Greetings, Obodai," Grandmother called out. "Did you get a good catch?"

"Greetings, old mother," Obodai said swinging his basket down to show her. "Better than yesterday. Here, Comfort, take these to Ata," he counted out a portion of his silvery load into Comfort's arms, keeping some for his second wife and some to sell. Comfort and Grandmother walked on into the village and stopped at the loud rumble of pottery wheels.

"Good evening, Sika," Grandmother called and the wheels rumbled slowly into silence. "Good evening, Kwame." Sika had come to the door, Kwame stood just behind him. Comfort fixed her eyes on the fish in her arms.

"Good evening, old one. You have fine fish there, Comfort, have you been to the river?" Sika said.

"We have been to Joshua's farm," Grandmother said.

"Aye-aye …" Sika shook his head. "Things are bad there, I am told."

"You are told for true," Grandmother said. "He is a no-good farmer, that one. After the harvest the farm will have another name most likely."

"Comfort's farm?" Sika suggested with a high-pitched laugh, glancing from grandmother to Comfort. "Old Comfort's farm, isn't it, but there are yellow sunflowers in the young one's cloth."

"We shall see … we shall see," Grandmother

145

murmured. "Yellow for property, my granddaughter is business-clever." Comfort gave a quick look towards Kwame. He was gazing steadily in her direction.

"'Two crocodiles do not have enough space in one cave'?" Sika remarked and Grandmother laughed again.

"You speak wisely, Sika. Give our headman a fish, Comfort, and one for Kwame too."

"Thank you, old mother. You are generous." As Kwame took his fish his lips close to Comfort's ear whispered, "Tonight. The tree?"

There was fish and vegetable stew for the evening meal and plenty of chopping and pounding to do. Kwame, Comfort thought, what would he say, what would she? The questions tumbled in her mind as her hands worked busily. It was dark by the time it was ready and by the time it was eaten and the pots washed a waxing moon had slid into the sky.

Comfort seized a moment when Grandmother was talking to Ata and slipped out of the compound.

"Where are you going?" Tawia called following her. "Can I come with you?" Comfort side-stepped quickly into a patch of deep shadow by the fence. "Comfort …" Tawia whispered passing so close they almost touched. Comfort held her breath. Tawia stopped, clicked her tongue irritably and turned back to the compound, not caring to walk alone in the ghost-filled darkness.

Comfort skirted the village, keeping away from the circles of light round the fires and pressure lamps hung in trees, the places where people gathered to talk after their meal.

Cicadas sang in the grass and an owl hooted as she followed the path she had taken with Grandmother earlier.

"Kwame?" she whispered. She couldn't see him but she knew he was there, the aroma of rose talcum flavoured the dark air like the Albertine and Fragrant Cloud in Grandad's garden. "Kwame?" His outline detached itself from the dark trunk of the tree.

"Greetings, Comfort." His voice was low, not the same as it had been, strange, a man's voice. Her heart was pounding as if it wanted to leap from her chest. "Shall we sit in the tree? You remember our tree?"

"Yes ... no ... they call it Kwame's tree, don't they?" Comfort stammered breathless. "Tawia says all the girls in Wanwangeri know Kwame's tree."

"Do they?" Kwame laughed pleased and complacent. "And perhaps Joshua's farm will soon be called Comfort's farm?"

"Not my farm," Comfort said quickly. "My grandmother's farm."

"If my father visits your grandmother soon, what will she say?" Kwame asked. She could see his eyes now under the moon but could not make out his expression. His hand held her arm, fingers stroking soft as petals.

"I don't know," she whispered breathlessly. "How could I?"

"Because it is your answer, isn't it?" Kwame whispered. "Though it comes from your grandmother's lips."

"Well ..." Comfort whispered. She couldn't pretend not to understand any more. "Well ... I'm only here for a month ..."

147

"We could kiss," Kwame said, his voice on a higher note. "They show films night-time in the lorry park of Akwapawa. I know how people kiss."

"Well …" Comfort said wanting and not wanting. "Well … I …" He leaned forward and brushed his lips against hers like a moth fluttering against a lamp and then his arms folded round her, muscular and strong. "If my father comes to your grandmother's compound, what answer will she give?" he whispered urgently.

"I've got to go now." Comfort broke out of the circle of his arms like a chick from an egg. "I'm only here for a month …" She ran back to the village. The compound was quiet, the children sleeping, Esi and Ata close to the hearth, talking in low voices. Nobody saw Comfort slip into her hut. She lay down on her bed a moment later, surprised to find her eyes were full of tears.

Me and Kwame talked, Comfort added to August 24th, watching her hands cross the page. Her writing was less straggly, she thought, more steady, more mature. *We shan't talk again. Not ever.*

When she returned to the market again Comfort had been quite exhilarated. Grandmother had changed her mind and when the market mammies heard that *Dry Leaf Fall* was going to Kumasi, it would surely be like the old days, she thought, friendly and full of laughter. She laid the cloth out on the stall as attractively as she could, calling out, "Buy my fine-fine cloth," and "Very cheap price," quite automatically, but half her attention was focussed on Ata leaning across Abla's stall and whispering. Comfort could not hear words but she could see the whisper going through the market like fire running through dry grass and could tell just how far it had got by the brightness in the cloth-sellers' eyes, squeals of high-pitched laughter and an air of suppressed excitement.

"Why does it have to be kept secret?" Comfort asked in an ordinary voice when Ata returned. Monopolies were bad, everyone said so and they had done monopolies at Lodge School only last term. So breaking them had to be good surely. "If Abdul got to know he might bring his prices down straight away."

"Hush," whispered Ata glancing over her shoulder. "You speak for true but Abdul is a big man ... when big men get angry, bad things can happen."

"Like what?" Comfort asked.

"Hush," whispered Ata glancing over her shoulder. "You speak for true but Abdul has a big family, lots of veranda boys who do what he says ... We are not wanting damage to *Dry Leaf Fall*, for instance?" Ata said. "The tyres slashed."

"Surely he wouldn't?" Comfort whispered shocked.

"Best to keep quiet," Ata had shrugged. "'To lose an elephant for a wren is foolish'."

Comfort's eyes circled the market. It was hard to believe such things could happen in Akwapawa when people seemed so open and the daylight so bright, even harder with the metal roof making the market air oven-hot and half the stall holders settled to a reassuring midday somnolence.

Baby born at last, she wrote and paused to dream-see the little thing, fawn with a mauvish tinge, the tiny fists flailing. Just thinking about the baby filled her with yearning and her mouth with spit. Had Margaret felt like that when she was born. Had Mante.

I have two little brothers now. Two stepbrothers. Half-Ga and half-Ashanti but both pure African. The boys would grow up in Ghana and even if they went to England as Mante had, always know where they belonged. How she would love to see them. She wanted to see the baby, of course, everybody wanted to see new babies even in Africa where there were so many, especially in Africa, but more than anything she wanted to see Jeo. Comfort rubbed her finger along the banana leaf in which her lunch of roast plantain and chillies had been wrapped and licked the trace of burning red juice. Surely there was some way she could get to Krempepong.

Two days later when Comfort and Ata returned to Wanwangeri, the children ran out to meet them bright-eyed with importance.

"Sad news."

"Talking drums bring bad news."

"Mante's wife does not choose right names."

"Grandmother very angry," they chorussed all together. Only little Kwashi was silent. Ata lifted him onto her hip. In the compound Grandmother was walking up and down the apron of concrete in front of her hut, muttering to herself.

"The flying-in-the-air woman, what does she know of our customs?" she demanded of the children who had run back to hear the full development of the drama.

"Nothing … nothing …" they chorussed obligingly.

"What is the trouble, old one, my mother?" Ata inquired.

"Am I just an old sponge to be flung aside?" Grandmother began. "The second boy in our family is called Aryan, so it has always been ... so it will always be ... for generation after generation ... but the Ashanti flying-in the-air woman says Jerry Kofi is to be his name. Jerry Kofi the talking drums say."

"Kofi is the name of Friday," Tawia ever helpful whispered to Comfort.

"Tell her Anan. Anan is the child's name, I say, and Tete sends the message for me again and again. Anan ... Anan ... but the flying-in-the-air woman takes no notice."

"Could he be called Anan Jerry Kofi then?" Comfort suggested. Like a tennis match, she thought, the children's eyes going back and forth between them.

"Anan Jerry Kofi," they muttered to each other.

"Anan is his name," Grandmother said. "So it has always been. This amulet to keep him safe once he is *outdoored*, I send to Anan and no other."

"Perhaps ..." Comfort began staring at the ground and trying to keep any provoking eagerness out of her voice. "Perhaps if I went to Krempepong on the lorry ... I could tell her the child was Anan ... explain properly ... give her the message and the amulet. Perhaps Efua doesn't read the talking drums."

"Only a month ... only a month you say you stay," Grandmother pointed her stick at the sky still pink and yellow where the sun had only just gone down. "Full moon when you come but it is not full moon again yet. Aye-aye ... a granddaughter sent by Onyame to be my ears and eyes ... a been-to granddaughter sent to help with the cloth business ..."

"If you let me go to Krempepong, I will be back by the full moon," Comfort said firmly. "I promise to come back to Wanwangeri."

"Besides, Mante will there for the outdooring ceremony," Ata said. "'The only palm fruit does not get lost in the fire', Comfort will keep her promise and Mante can bring her back."

"Keep her promise, keep her promise," the children echoed.

"Go then," Grandmother said. "Go with the lorry on Sunday, only let the child be called Anan."

Chapter 12

Dry Leaf Fall rattled down the road in the direction of Kumasi. The bookman sat beside the driver and Comfort and Ata and ten market women including Abla and Dede sat in the back. It was already hot. The driver had not welcomed the loss of his free Sunday, the dignity of his skilled status was threatened by the machinations of the market mammies. *Fear Woman* was rightly said. He had already subjected *Dry Leaf Fall* to its Sunday morning ablutions, hosing away the week's accumulation of dust and revealing a bonnet green as lettuce and yellow as lemon. The lorry still dripped but wet seats would soon dry in the heat.

"You know the cloth warehouse?" Ata said in English as they set off. "You know the way?"

"Warehouse, him close Sunday," the driver said sulkily, distancing himself from the foolhardy scheme.

"Warehouse man wait there for us," Abla said. "We telephone,"

"Stop first at the lorry park outside, Comfort go

for Krempepong," Ata had added.

There was an exultant ripple through the market women as the lorry set off. Soon they would have cloth at a fair price, they patted their waists for reassurance, feeling the money knotted into their cloths. Abdul would bring down his prices, and if he didn't they would go to Kumasi again until he did. Past miseries were as easily discarded as old clothes in the brilliant sunshine.

Comfort smoothed her newly-washed cloth over her knees, her bundle lay between her feet. She was going to Krempepong, she would see Jeo and the new baby and Efua and Mante too when he came for the outdooring ceremony of his second son. Her head was stuffed like a turkey with messages and good wishes for the baby and her bundle contained Grandmother's amulet and presents from Ata and Esi as well as Lambkin. 'Comfort Jones, you have a long way to go,' she fingered Margaret's ring through her cloth. She was Comfort Kwatey-Jones now but she still had a long way to go. The journey to Krempepong was what she wanted, what she had carefully negotiated, but now she was on her way a flutter of apprehension nagged her stomach and her mouth felt dry. Krempepong was Ashanti land and nobody else knew she had Ashanti blood. An oblong of blue had shown on the map, Krempepong Lake, "Anan ... Anan ..." she murmured under her breath. The market women chatted and joked all round her, shouting above the rattle of the lorry, ebullience restored by the day out and the better turn of events and for a moment Comfort longed to stay with them.

"Couldn't I go to the warehouse for the cloth with you first?" she said to Ata.

"What for?" Ata asked. "We reach the Kumasi lorry park first, so you will be in Krempepong before the midday heat."

"But if ..." Comfort began uncertainly.

"No ifs ... you can take sick and die of ifs." Ata's laugh rumbled through her body. "The tro-tro bus goes every hour. You have money for the tro-tro bus? Better get there while it is cool. What can go wrong?" Ata said, used to travelling and infinitely gregarious. "Tete sent the message. They are expecting you at Krempepong."

"Yes," Comfort said scolding herself. Hadn't she insisted to Granny in Penfold that she was perfectly able to travel to Folkestone by herself. Krempepong was only five kilometres from Kumasi and she was fourteen after all. Fourteen was grown-up in Wanwangeri, Ata had been married and with child by fourteen. What was Kwame doing now, she wondered, but dismissed it. Kwame and his leafy tree. She wasn't going to think about Kwame.

She looked quickly out at the forest on either side, deep pools of shade and patterns of light where the sun penetrated the green ceiling of trees gradually giving way to patches of cultivation, villages, and then the shanty dwellings which surround most African towns. Then the wider streets of Kumasi with high graceful buildings on either side and people thronging the streets ready for church and the tolling of bells.

"This Kumasi." The driver, who had kept his silence, resisting the attempts of the women to draw him into their lively banter, jumped down now and opened the back flap of the lorry. "This Kumasi lorry park."

"Goodbye, Comfort," the women called as *Dry*

Leaf Fall pulled away, pale-palmed hands waving in the shadow of the lorry like flowers in the wind. "Goodbye, Comfort."

"Where tro-tro bus?" Comfort said so softly nobody heard. All round her people were talking in Twi and she understood only the occasional familiar word and the rest was incomprehensible babble. "White girl, white girl," Manko's taunts and slapping hand rang in her head and panic gripped her. Her hand clutched the ring at her neck, Margaret's ring.

"Where tro-tro bus for Krempepong?" Comfort said louder.

"There, there," people pointed smiling and incurious. A light-skinned girl in Ghanaian cloth, there were many such girls in Kumasi and other big towns where Europeans came and went on short-term contracts.

An hour later she stepped down from the tro-tro bus blinking in the sudden brightness, leaving the pitted tarmac road for the sandy track which led to Krempepong. Faraway a drum throbbed in the hot air. Was it a message, Comfort wondered.

It was good to be out of the stifling heat of the bus and in the shade of trees but the track was deeply rutted, trapping her feet and she moved onto the grassy verge where her sandals made no sound. The village wasn't far, already she could hear the shout of distant voices and see smoke rising.

Suddenly the trees thinned and Comfort saw water shining between the trunks, the lake sapphire blue under the sun and then she was out of the trees altogether and Krempepong lay below her in a saucer of land beside the lake. She stood still taking it all in. A cluster of houses and fences, square houses with metal roofs and front verandas, Krempepong was a larger and more affluent village than Wanwangeri. On the far side of the lake there were more houses, another village.

Something rustled nearby and Comfort's eyes turned towards the bushes. A girl was kneeling there, a wide-eyed girl in a dark blue cloth.

"Peace?" Comfort said; the girl stood up, startled but didn't answer. "Peace, you are Peace, aren't you?"

The girl turned and ran wildly through the grass and bushes towards the lake and the path that edged it, disappearing between the trees.

Comfort walked on more slowly. Was it Peace, she couldn't be sure after so long or perhaps Peace had a sister. Several small boys in twists of printed cloth were running towards her as she approached the village, laughing as they ran, but then stopped and stared, suddenly shy.

"Greetings," Comfort said scanning their faces eagerly. "Jeo? Do you know Jeo, my little brother?" She patted the air with her hand to indicate his height. The children stared at her but didn't answer. Was it her Twi they didn't understand, she wondered. "Jeo? Jeo?"

They shook their heads, joined by several other children, laughing again, safety in numbers.

"This village is Krempepong?" she asked uncertainly.

"Yes, yes, Krempepong Major," a dozen heads nodded.

"Jeo?" Comfort tried again. "Do you know where my brother Jeo is?"

"No, no, no," the children shook their heads, capering round her like the Pied Piper, as she walked into the village. A red car was parked close to a compound fence, a sleeping mat spread to protect the roof. A surge of relief, she knew that car like an old friend though she had never seen it, only the tyre marks it had made, angry tyre marks. But at least Efua was somewhere near. The drumming was louder now.

"Greetings, Comfort Kwatey-Jones. Welcome to Krempepong Major." A woman had come out from one of the compounds, a middle-aged woman with a dark green cloth, a calm and responsible air and a great many gold bracelets. She spoke slowly and carefully in Twi. "I am Ya. You must be tired from your journey? Come inside and drink." Comfort followed her through the fence leaving the retinue of children behind. The whole compound was floored with white concrete, gleaming white in the hot sun. She led Comfort to one of the larger huts with a wide veranda in front.

"Bring drink," she called to the shadowy doorway as they settled on two stools. The sound of fufu pounded and smells of cooking came from behind the hut, despite the early hour and the heat of the day.

"Where are Jeo and Peace and Efua?" Comfort asked haltingly.

"Jeo and Peace …" Ya murmured, mouthing the words as if they were sweets she didn't much like. She glanced in the direction of the lake, little points of blue were visible between the palm fronds of the fence.

"Efua is my stepmother … I must see Efua," Comfort said in English louder than was quite polite. "I've come to see Efua and the new baby. I have a message for Efua."

"Efua is here," Ya said gesturing towards another hut still speaking in Twi but evidently understanding English. "Tomorrow the child will be outdoored, tomorrow you can see them. Already we prepare food for the many guests."

"But I ... I must see them before that," Comfort said getting to her feet with a rising sense of desperation. The drumming had stopped.

"It is not the custom," Ya said with calm finality. "Do you want to bring the child bad luck? You can sleep in my hut tonight. Tomorrow you can see them, after the ceremony."

"But I have a message," Comfort said and her voice rang out in the midday quiet. "I must see Efua ... I must ..."

"Comfort, my daughter ..." Efua was standing in the doorway of the furthest hut, tall, authoritative and beautiful, her leopard-patterned cloth wound under her armpits like any village woman. "Let her come, Ya."

"It is not the custom ..." Ya grumbled but Comfort was already running across the hot white concrete.

"Such old-fangled nonsense, Ya has never left this village," Efua explained folding Comfort in her arms and then standing back, appraising, smiling. And Comfort looked at Efua too, the same proud nostrils, the same carnelian eyes but there was something different, something softer, not just the fullness of her body. Efua had lost her air of perpetual discontent, there was a new tranquillity about her, a new tenderness.

"The drums told me you are coming. Come and see my little son," Efua said, and Comfort followed her into the dimness of the hut where the baby lay in a basket, swaddled in a dark blue cloth and fast asleep.

"Beautiful ... a fine-fine son ..." Comfort whispered laying one finger on the tiny whorled ear. "He looks like Mante, doesn't he?" Jeo had been hospital born, slept on a blue organdie pillow in a white cot and had Paddington Bear on his curtains. "Where's Jeo?"

"Oh, Jeo ... somewhere about ..." Efua said with something of the same tone Ya had used "Such a troublesome child ... a true Ashanti ..." she smiled at the admission. "Always restless ... whining ... cry-cry all night ... the *adehye* blood is restless, they say, but in this place he does well. Krempepong suits Jeo. Besides ..." Efua hesitated a moment. "One day my brother will be chief of Krempepong and Jeo is his heir."

"Jeo? Doesn't your brother have children then?" Comfort said.

"Of course ..." Efua shrugged impatiently. "Plenty of children but no man can be quite certain that his child is his and has the *adeyhe* blood, can he? That is why the chieftaincy goes through the female line, Jeo has my royal blood."

"And what about Anan?" Comfort whispered.

"This one, this sleep-sleep baby ... this very good boy," Efua said lovingly. She picked up the baby then, as if she could hardly bear separation any longer and tied the still sleeping child onto her back, something she had never done with Jeo. "For seven days we have been alone together ... this baby and me ... everything quiet like the womb ... everything peaceful ... so we get to know each other. I do not want any hospital place with clatter and rushing. Aye-aye ... I am glad to see you,

Comfort." Efua finished embracing her again and again, holding her at arm's length. "You are Mante's child too, that is certain, you look so like him. Tell me what is happening in the world outside. I have been alone in Krempepong too long, alone in this hut, but tomorrow is the outdooring. Mante is coming for the ceremony, coming to greet this new Ga child."

"Grandmother sends her blessings, and this amulet," Comfort said and hesitated not wanting to spoil things, the new accord between them, but Anan was what she had come for. "She says ... she says the second son is always Anan in our family."

"Chu, Anan ..." Efua moved restlessly up and down the hut. "Such an old-fangled name ... Jerry I thought ... after the big man ... it is good to have a big man's name ... 'When there is a big tree small ones climb on its back to reach the sun'."

"But Anan is a good name," Comfort said urgently. "I have come a long way to tell you Anan. It is good to keep the customs, Grandmother says, barbarians and animals have no customs."

"What for you cross-talk me?" Carnelian eyes with their reddish tinge glared fiercely at Comfort.

"Sorry ... sorry," Comfort whispered. There was a pause and suddenly Efua flung back her head and laughed, a full-throated joyous laugh.

"What does it matter? Let him be outdoored as Anan then," she said. "Anan Jerry, but I shall call him Jerry. Oh, you are a good girl, Comfort, and I shall call him Anan just for you. You're pretty too, a beautiful young woman in your red and yellow cloth ... your father should be proud of you."

"Couldn't you ... I mean couldn't you be a bit proud of me too?" Comfort said shyly.

Chapter 13

"Jeo?" Comfort whispered, sleeping and dreaming, searching through empty houses in empty streets, the front door slamming and Mante gone, Margaret gone, Ruby gone … Joshua … walking and whispering. "Jeo? Where are you? Anan …?"

Comfort was lying on a sleeping mat in Ya's hut where she had slept the night with Ya and the other women who had attended the birth of Efua's baby but now she was alone. Brilliant white light filled the doorway and beyond the other mats lay out in the sun and the women had gone. Today was outdooring day and all round the sounds of preparation had begun, shouts and laughter, knives chopping on wood, the crackle of fire in sticks. Hens pecked in the dust and dogs wandered where there might be food.

Somewhere beyond the fence a talking drum beat softly. What was it saying, Comfort wondered, announcing the outdooring or that Mante was expected soon. If only she could read the talking drums, hear the eagle's cry and the frog's croak and the leopard's growl. Was it because of her English blood that she couldn't hear them. Perhaps Grandmother would teach her or perhaps it would suddenly come like learning to swim. Anan, she had succeeded in that at least, the baby was going to be outdoored as Anan. And Efua had been really pleased to see her. Stepmothers were always wicked in Chinese and English fairy tales, Maxine said, but perhaps Ghanaian fairy tales were different.

"Greetings, Comfort, and good morning," Ya said, gathered at the food store with the older women but supervising the chopping and cooking and already wearing a handsome cloth of peacock-blue and many gold bracelets to signify her importance as woman and midwife on this particular occasion. "What will you eat? Your father is arriving soon for the outdooring."

"What about Jeo? I must find Jeo, nobody seems to know where Jeo and Peace are but they can't just disappear into thin air, can they?" Comfort said with an uneasy little laugh, knowing asking such a question was a not-done thing, aware that faces had changed all round her, lengthening and becoming expressionless, just as they had the night before.

"Oh, Jeo …" they murmured vaguely. "Jeo … "

"Is he sick or something?" Comfort said.

"Not all questions are good," Ya said coolly. "It is not polite for visitors to worry-worry at such matters like a dog with a bone."

"But what else can I do? Jeo is my brother and my father is coming today," Comfort said exasperated, looking across at Efua's hut but she wouldn't be allowed in there again. "He will want to take Jeo home."

"Perhaps …" said Ya turning her back so briskly

that her bracelets jingled and walking away to Efua's hut. Comfort looked after the peacock-blue figure but knew better than to follow. Something was going on but what, and why wouldn't they tell her? It might not be polite for visitors to worry-worry but it wasn't all that polite to worry-worry the visitors either. Anyway she wasn't a visitor, she was one-sixteenth Ashanti and it wasn't her fault she didn't know the not-done Ashanti thing and Jeo was her brother. Comfort tucked Lambkin into her cloth and walked through the village towards the lake. Several children came running after her. Cocoa farming was evidently the chief activity at Krempepong Major. Dark-leaved cocoa trees encircled the village and small patches had even pushed their way between the outlying huts, the great pods hanging almost ready for harvest.

"Ah, Comfort, child of Mante ... greetings, Comfort," people called in Twi, standing at the doors of compounds or working along the cocoa trees. "You have come for the outdooring of your brother? That is good."

"Yes," said Comfort "I have come for the outdooring but where is Jeo, my other brother? Have you seen Jeo?"

Faces grew blank just as she had anticipated, heads shook vaguely, eyes looked away. Nobody was going to tell her but what was it that they weren't going to tell.

By the time she reached the lake a dozen children were following her. "Do you know Jeo? Where is Jeo? And Peace?" Comfort asked them, swinging round and watching as twelve small faces went blank, the children melting away in twos and threes just as they had come. She gazed across the turquoise-blue water, oval-shaped but long like a cucumber dish rimmed round with a white path where Peace had run, a long blue dish with a white rim dropped by a giant hand and lying where it fell amongst dark-green cocoa trees and lighter green forest. Several small rafts lay on the shore above the water line but no canoes. Odd, Comfort thought, looking across to the other side where there seemed to be another smaller village. It wasn't far. She would like to go across.

A stick cracked and a little boy wandered from the bushes and stood staring at her.

"Hello," she whispered, bending down to the child's level. He was smaller than Jeo, about two years old. "What's your name?"

"Ayi," the child whispered close to her ear.

"Ayi, that's a nice name," Comfort said. "Do you know Jeo? Jeo and Peace, where are they?" The boy regarded her solemnly for a moment and then raised his arm, pointing across the lake towards the group of huts the other side. Comfort knew then what Ya's straying glance had hinted and Peace's flight had already told her.

"What you want, you?" A much bigger boy in a knotted red cloth had come along the path. The question was in English but he dropped into Twi scolding the little boy whose arm fell back to his side; he burst into tears and ran away. "What for you come to this place?" the older boy demanded frowning. He was taller and a bit older than Comfort.

"Nothing," she said. "I was just looking at the rafts ... Is one of them yours, I mean could you take me across?"

There was a sharp intake of breath, the boy's eyes widened with alarm. "Not fit ..." he said. "Women ...

girls ... not fit for lake. Not come ... go away."

"What do you mean 'not fit'?" Comfort said, not sure it was appropriate to get indignant. "I can paddle a canoe quite well ... and swim ..."

"Not fit ... not fit ..." the boy repeated fiercely, more alarmed than ever, and bitterly frustrated by his small command of English. "Old man, the lake, him not like canoe, him say only raft fit for lake."

"But why ..."

"It is the custom." The boy's face was stony. "Lake, him not like canoe. Fish, him not like womans ... females ..."

"So how can I get across?"

"Not go ... Krempepong Minor not good place for you ... you go away, you," the boy muttered walking away with a last nervous glance across the smooth surface of the water.

Comfort stood for a moment. She knew now that everybody else in Krempepong had seemed to know but would not tell her, that Jeo was on the other side of the lake. And she knew too what she had to do. If she couldn't get across, she would have to go round. If Peace could walk round so could she but the outdooring ceremony would be early evening and she had to find Jeo before that. She set off following the hard white path.

Behind her a drum began to beat. What was it saying now, the cry of an eagle, the croak of a frog or was it telling the tale of the boy by the lake. Had he seen her go? Had anyone? Would they try to stop her? Comfort glanced over her shoulder and walked faster. In the dust there were marks, the half-prints of Peace's running feet becoming full prints as her pace had slowed to walk. Cocoa trees were far behind now. Not many people followed the path so far out of the village, so far into the forest, and birds squawked stridently, resenting the intrusion, lizards scuttled and snakes slithered discreetly, black and green. The green mamba was very poisonous and Comfort waited until long after it had gone.

It was hot and the sun high by the time she reached the strip of marshy land either side of the stream which fed the lake and knew she was halfway. She jumped the stream and sat on a fallen tree to rest a moment. She was very thirsty and the water looked clean enough but Mante had told her about bilharzia and typhoid and river blindness and she knew better than to drink it. She could see both villages equally well now, the food preparation going on in Krempepong Major, smoke rising and people hurrying about. Krempepong Minor had the same square huts, mud-walled and iron-roofed, and a central banyan tree. People were coming and going there, too, but nobody hurried in the heat of the day. Halfway between the villages, Comfort thought, just as she was suspended like a trapeze artist halfway between Ghana and England, black and white, Grandmother and Granny, Folkestone and Penfold, a society which taught girls to canoe on lakes and one which denied them the chance. A water snake wriggled to the surface of the lake and sank out of sight again. Comfort wiped her face on the edge of her cloth and walked on.

It was still hotter when she reached the far side of the lake and Krempepong Minor seemed almost deserted. She had walked some three kilometres in the heat of the day and now she walked slowly, blue water glittering and the sand burning her feet even through her sandals. A dog barked as she approached and a small child came to a hut door, stared in her direction and then melted back into the darkness.

Comfort sat down in the shade of the banyan tree. Did they know she was coming? Had the talking drum told them? Slowly, very slowly, children emerged from their huts whispering and creeping forward to stand in a big circle round her.

"Hallo," Comfort said in Twi.

"Hallo," the children answered.

"Which of you is Jeo?" she asked. Twenty children, more boys than girls and at least six were the right age but all the children shook their heads.

"No, no, no ..." they glanced towards the huts as if for approval.

"Do you know Jeo?" Comfort asked.

"Don't know ... don't know ... don't know ...' the children chorused, shaking their heads. Comfort pulled Lambkin from her cloth lizard-quick and held it up. Twenty pairs of eyes stared at the white woolly lamb.

"Mine," a little boy said in English and stretched out his hands and ran forward. "Lambkin ... Lambkin ... mine."

"Jeo ... you're Jeo," Comfort said putting Lambkin into his arms. Hot tears pricked the back of her eyes. She could see it was Jeo now that she knew. He was so like Efua, the flare of his nostrils and the carnelian tinge to the colour of his eyes. "You're my brother Jeo."

"No, no, no," Peace came running towards them, grabbing Jeo and pulling Lambkin out of his hands. "No want, no want. This boy not Jeo, this boy Kofi." Jeo began to scream.

"Stop it, stop it," Comfort shouted grabbing Lambkin too. "Let him have it, Peace."

A melée then. Two girls fighting in the hot sun, grabbing, pulling hair, shouting, a tearing of cloth and Jeo in the middle screaming and screaming. People coming out of huts and running along paths towards the two girls fighting. Scolding in Twi and slapping, hands pulling them apart. Peace talking, pleading, everyone listening, eyes going back and forth, all of Krempepong Minor listening to Peace talking and Comfort not quite understanding.

"Wait," they said to Comfort leading her towards a hut. "You wait here, we fetch chief. Chief know what is right."

"Jeo is my brother," Comfort said over and over. "I must take him back for the outdooring. My father is coming …"

"Wait," they said. "You wait." It was a small square hut but different from the others with a high, thatched roof and a wide open window, unglazed, looking over the lake, mats and stools to sit on and water to drink. Later they brought her food, cold rice wrapped in a parcel of green leaf, roasted plantain and a handful of groundnuts.

"But my father is coming," Comfort said despairingly. Time was passing. "He will be here soon for the outdooring, the new baby, I must take Jeo back."

"Chief does not hurry," They said calmly. "Chief soon fix quarrel."

"But the outdooring … Anan's outdooring …"

"You can go," they suggested. "Just leave the boy you call your brother and go."

But Comfort couldn't go. Even if she missed the outdooring, she couldn't leave Jeo in Krempepong Minor now she had found him. Jeo himself had gone back to play 'cars' with the other children under the banyan tree. Comfort sat at the window staring across the lake, darker blue now as the sun slid down from its zenith. She considered the rafts drawn up on the shore, small rafts made of wood lashed together and perched on top of two oil drums. On the other side of the lake 'the pace of activity quickened even more, people hurrying, women running in and out of different huts. Above the village and far away she could see the main road where she had left the tro-tro bus and the track leading off it where she had walked and first seen Peace. Presently she saw a car driving along the track, a white car coated in thick pink dust, disappearing behind cocoa trees, reappearing and finally arriving at the village. Instantly it was surrounded by children, jumping, laughing, touching. Not many cars came to Krempepong. Her father got out, tall and dignified, in his kente cloth worn like a toga, the silk shining in the sun.

"Mante," Comfort called loud as she could, leaning out of the hut. "Mante." Her voice went spinning across the water like a scudding stone. For an instant he paused, turned his head and looked across the lake. "Mante," Comfort called again high above the drum, waving both her arms. But Ya had come out to greet him and people were talking all round, he was walking on, disappearing behind a compound fence.

"Oh, Jeo," Comfort said turning at a slight noise behind her. Evidently the boy had heard her call. He stood doubtfully in the doorway with Lambkin in one hand and a long stick with a tin lid nailed to the end, his car, in the other.

He was freshly bathed and wore a striped red and cream cloth knotted behind his neck, new and unfaded by the sun. He was better dressed than the other children. At least Peace looked after him.

"Come in, Jeo," Comfort said in English. "I'm your sister, Comfort, aren't I?" Jeo stared at her solemnly but didn't move and she tried again in Twi. She longed to cuddle him, hold him tight against her, this little boy she had thought so much about, made Lambkin for, and come such a long way to find. 'Comfort Jones you have a long way to go.' But Jeo slid away from her arms not caring to be cuddled, staring at her with eyes so like Efua's. Ashanti eyes full of fierceness.

"Sister …" he said suddenly in English, pointing his finger. "I see photograph."

"That's right," Comfort said happily. "Look Daddy … over there." He allowed her to lift him up to the window space, staring across the lake where she was pointing.

"Papa …" he said pointing too, smiling and finding the spectacle across the lake diverting for the moment. People had gathered in the middle of the village now, some wearing silk kente, other bright new cotton cloths, the priest in white. They moved towards Ya's compound.

"Mama …" Jeo murmured as Efua came out of her hut with the baby in her arms. There was chanting and libations were poured on the ground, north, south, east, west to the ancestors and Gods of the Ashanti people, the sky-family thanked for letting the child come to earth again and for letting him stay, Anan Jerry, the second son of Mante Kwatey-Jones. Then the solemn moment was over, people crowded round, passing the child from one to another. Drumming started up again.

"Baby ..." Comfort said. "Your little brother, Anan." She had seen the outdooring even though she missed it. Had Grandmother heard the drum message yet, she wondered. Did she know the child was correctly named?

"Car ..." said Jeo wanting to get down now. He pushed his stick along the floor so the tin lid turned like a wheel and went out of the door. "Car."

It was early evening and the lake was inky-blue when the chief and his adviser finally arrived. The chief was an old man, quite small and bent, clad in leopard skin with a circle of thick gold discs round his head and another round his neck and gold bands at knees and ankles hung with little bells which jingled as he walked. His adviser walked beside him and behind were two young men, one carrying two stools, the other holding a huge scarlet umbrella above the chief. They settled under the banyan tree and Comfort was called.

"Comfort Kwatey-Jones," the adviser inquired severely. "Why have you come to Krempepong Minor and disturbed our people?"

"Please ... please," Comfort said breathlessly, knees shaking, looking from one to the other not sure who to address or whether she had quite understood. Peace and Jeo stood beside her and the rest of the village sat on the ground behind. "Please ... I came to fetch my little brother Jeo, and take him home."

"He stay ... he stay here," Peace shouted.

"Quiet, girl," the adviser commanded. "Did your father send you for the child?"

"No ... no ... my father has only just arrived at

Krempepong Major," she pointed across the lake deep violet now with a round red patch of reflected sun. "For the outdooring ..."

"Your father ..." the chief spoke in English clipped and clear, he gazed across the lake where lights twinkled in the trees and the feasting had started. "Your father can fetch the child if he wants surely?"

"Yes, but I thought ..." the words died away. There was something about the chief's eyes, a dark gaze so penetrating that it was hardly necessary to tell him what she had thought, because he already knew.

"Hear me, Comfort," he said. "It is best that the boy stays here. Do you know of his lineage?"

"I know ... I know he has *adehye* blood," Comfort said.

"Aye-aye ... *adehye* blood," the people of the village murmured picking up the word they knew from much they could not follow, understanding pidgin English better than standard.

"*Adehye* blood indeed," the chief said with a proud little smile. Jeo ran forward and scrambled on to his knee with Peace trying to restrain him. "Let him be," the chief said holding Jeo against him. "Jeo had my blood, royal blood. When I was a boy they sent me to famous school in England, Clifton College, because of my *adehye* blood but been-to and *adehye* do not mix. Aye-aye ... I learn Greek and Latin and team spirit and house colours and run the 'long pen' and my friend is Smithson Minor and my hero is Smithson Major but I forget the ways of my people ..." he shook his head sadly. "I am no use to my people for many years when I return ... no use at all ... My nephew is the next chief, my sister's child. It is the way we do things in our tribe ... women being occasionally perfidious ... only a sister's child is certain to carry the *adehye* blood. My nephew is been-to schooled, a paediatrician much respected in Accra but the people's hearts are heavy with an absent chief."

"Aye-aye ... an absent chief is grievous thing," the village people murmured to one another.

"Do you hear me, Comfort?"

"I hear you," Comfort said slowly, her confidence returning and her voice quite steady now. Never be frightened by words, Margaret said. "But ... but ... I do not have to agree with you, do I?"

There was a hiss of shock from the villagers behind. "Be silent, Comfort Kwatey-Jones," the adviser said sternly.

"Let her speak," the chief said.

"All I want is Jeo, to take Jeo back," Comfort said.

"Jeo ... Jeo ..." the village people murmured.

"Jeo is my nephew's nephew, his sister's child," the chief said. "Perhaps ... I only say perhaps ... it is best that he stays here where he belongs. He can be schooled in Kumasi and live for some time at the Asantehene's palace and learn the ancient customs as the old chiefs used to do. Perhaps that is the education this boy needs ... this restless Ashanti boy." He gently tweaked Jeo's ear. "His mother thinks so too."

"But his father ..." Comfort swallowed. Everything was slipping away, the long walk round the lake, everything she had come for, Jeo. "But my father is Ga, Jeo is half-Ga."

"I know, I know ... such things happen unfortunately," the chief murmured.

"And a child should be with his parents surely ... it is where he belongs?" Comfort said.

"Who can say?" the chief observed setting Jeo upon his feet again. "Certainly if his parents come and fetch him the boy must go. But you cannot take him, Comfort, what does a half-white girl from boarding school in England know of such things?" He turned his eyes towards Krempepong Major, a ball of light on the far side of the dark lake, where drumming and dancing had started. "A child belongs to his family, but a chief belongs to his people. So it has always been."

Chapter 14

It was almost dark when Comfort set off along the lake path. "Stay," they said. "Stay here for the night, it will be dark soon."

"Ghosts," murmured Peace, solicitous now that the chief had given in her favour, holding Jeo tight in her arms and wanting to be forgiven. "Ghosts walk at night."

"What ghosts?" Comfort had said. Ghosts came out of a person's own psyche, Miss Beale said. Ghosts were just nerves or indigestion, Granny said, despising both but keeping away from churchyards just the same. "I'd better go," Comfort had said glancing towards the lake, dark-mauve like deadly night-shade now under the darkening sky but the path still showed white.

She didn't want to stay without Jeo, if she couldn't have Jeo, he was what she had come for after all. The outdooring festivities were still going on, would go on far into the night and the fires of Krempepong Major and the pressure lamps hanging in the trees made a haven of yellow light that drew her back like a moth. The lights of Krempepong Major would keep away ghosts at least until the moon came up. Besides she had to get back to Mante as fast as she could. Tell him everything, it was up to him to rescue Jeo. There was no road into Krempepong Minor as far as she could see but there must be some way of getting there. Mante would be in a hurry to get back to his office and she had to catch him before he left and bring him back to Krempepong Minor.

Comfort walked quickly at first, wanting to get as far as she could before it was quite dark. The path was clear but there were deep shadows under the trees now and scuttering and scampering. She kept her eyes on the water, its glassy surface occasionally broken by the plop of a leaping fish. Across the water the drumming and dancing went on in the patch of yellow light. But questions churned in Comfort's head and gradually her feet grew slower. Suppose they sent Jeo away somewhere straight away; to the Asantahene's palace, perhaps. Hadn't she seen a significant look pass between chief and adviser? Suppose there was no road to Krempepong Minor or Mante had left before she even got round the lake? Suppose Jeo was lost for ever, they would not blame her with words but their eyes would blame her, black eyes and carnelian. How could she have left him, they would ask.

Comfort stopped and looked back at Krempepong Minor. A single pressure lamp hung in the banyan tree and shadowy figures stood at the edge of the lake, some watching the dancing, others executing small dances of their own in time to the drums. Below them the line of rafts pulled up along the shore.

Such a long way round, such a short distance across.

The pattern of everything, the purpose was becoming clear. Hadn't she always been a good swimmer, got her Life Saving Certificate last term, gone on that canoeing holiday last year? She leaned against a tree. Waiting. Waiting so long that small animals resumed their courses through the undergrowth and a snake slithered unheeding past her foot. Presently a party of dancers broke away from Krempepong Minor to join the revels on the far side. They came down the path very fast, keeping close together, talking and laughing.

Their eyes were fixed on the opposite lights and they didn't notice Comfort as they passed close by.

Comfort stayed where she was. What was she going to do? She didn't know. Not yet. She just knew she had to do it. Self-reliance, Mante said, self-reliance was the keyword in the new Ghana. A moon almost full rose into the sky making a broad road across the lake, white and glimmering, joining the two villages and still she waited. Krempepong Minor was quiet now, no lights showed but in Krempepong Major they were dancing still.

Comfort stood up making no sound but rubbing her stiff legs. She walked back towards the sleeping village and pushed the endmost raft onto the water, slowly and carefully. A faint scraping sound like a match on a box. There was no sense in hurrying. There was this thing she had to do and you could do anything you wanted, Margaret said, if you wanted to enough.

Comfort waded into the dark water, feeling the mud soft between her toes and lifting each foot carefully, pushing the raft before her. She picked up the paddle and then put one foot on the raft, scooting as hard as she could with the other foot, landing on top crouched on all fours, wobbling a precarious moment and then sitting down. "Oh." Getting her balance as the raft slid forward, teetering dangerously as one corner caught on the bottom and then lifted and steadied in the deeper water. She was afloat.

For a moment she sat there with her eyes shifting back and forth. Had the splash been heard? But nothing stirred in Krempepong Minor and in Krempepong Major the dancing still went on. She dipped the paddle, wobbling again and began to move slowly out onto the lake. Hot exultation flared inside her. All first time things you had to do by yourself, self-reliance, nobody could help you. Like first time swimming the length of the baths at Brixton, first bike ride down the road, first time she paddled her canoe right across the river Wye and everybody clapped. She could do it, she could do it … but now she damped the excitement.

The raft afloat was only the beginning. One step at a time, the canoe instructor said over and over.

She paddled slowly, dipping the paddle carefully, delicately making no sound until she reached the little beach of Krempepong Minor, deserted now. She pulled the raft half out of the water. One step at a time. Nothing stirred as she crept towards the huts, gun-metal grey under the moon, marking with her eyes the one she wanted, the hut where Jeo and Peace slept.

She stepped inside the doorway and stood there, the pounding of her heart was deafening and yet she could still hear quiet breathing on the floor below her. One step at a time. As her eyes got used to the darkness she made out the two forms, Jeo lay beside Peace, a cloth tucked round his body, dark cloth on light mat and the white patch of Lambkin gripped in his fist. She leaned down and lifted him in her arms, whispering softly, soothingly, he was heavier than she realised. She stepped out of the hut.

The moonlight seemed brighter now, so bright Comfort blinked and with Jeo in her arms she moved towards the lake, bending forward, gliding swiftly.

"Jeo, it's all right, Jeo," she whispered over and over but he didn't seem to have woken. She unwrapped her cloth, swinging him gently onto her back, pinpointing him there, swaddled and and fastened tight.

"Just for a bit, Jeo, just for a bit you can be my cloth baby, eh, Jeo? Don't be frightened." The water, cold and silky on her feet. She pushed the raft out onto the water.

Jeo woke then. She felt him move, start, and turning her head saw the whites of his eyes wide with fright but he made no sound. Not then. Did he think he was dreaming still, Comfort wondered.

"It's all right, Jeo," she scooted with one foot and just a she did so, a wail went up in the village behind her.

"Jeo, Jeo, Jeo." And then wild screaming.

Comfort pushed off hard and lunged onto the raft, rocking perilously with the extra burden of Jeo's weight. She slumped as low as she could and waited for the raft to steady beneath her and as she began to paddle Jeo began to scream. Behind her there was shouting. Lights. Comfort paddled furiously, splashing loud now while Jeo screamed on and on. "You're a big boy, Jeo. You're all right, Jeo."

The wide white path of the moon and fearful thoughts crowding, suppose they capsized, could she swim with Jeo on her back, Jeo screaming. Screaming and threshing against her back, small fists and Lambkin thumping.

Behind her lights moving in Krempepong Minor and people darting, running towards the shore where Peace stood shrieking, "Jeo, Jeo."

Jeo screamed louder. Frantic.

"Hush, Jeo, hush," Comfort said turning to pat him, making the raft rock. "Don't cry, don't cry." Cold tears on her own face too. A splash behind as another raft was launched. "Don't cry, don't cry."

A raft coming across the water, moving faster. How long before they reached her? What would they do, what would she. Comfort paddled desperately and from the shore heard a voice command in Twi, the voice of the chief's adviser. The other paddling ceased and the raft drifted where it was. Voices muttered angrily in the darkness as the raft turned slowly and paddled back. Jeo stopped crying then, a little shudder and then silence.

"Good boy, Jeo, Jeo my little brother," Comfort murmured over and over, like a chant. Hadn't she heard Peace singing to quieten him long ago?

She was in deep water now, the centre, the heart of the lake like black glass under the moon. What did he think, she wondered, the old man, the lake himself who did not care for girls and women, forbade them to come near him.

Her arms ached and the palms of her hands were burning and blistered but she was almost there now and aware suddenly that the dancing had stopped in Krempepong Major and people stood all along the shore, staring in her direction. Waiting. Soundless.

"I have Jeo," Comfort called in Twi, breaking the silence. Her voice went bouncing across the water but the people gave no sign of having heard. Now she was close enough to see them individually under the moon, Mante and Efua brilliant in their kente cloths, Ya holding the baby, Anan. But still nobody spoke. The raft nudged the shore and Comfort staggered onto her feet, untying her cloth. They came round her, gasping and exclaiming, hands plucking, taking Jeo up and carrying him away.

"Jeo, my son," Efua cried. "He is safe."

Everyone moved away from the lake shore then, everyone except Comfort and Mante. A wayward girl was first of all her father's problem, after that the headman would consider the case, the insult to the lake. Mante looked at Comfort for a long time.

"What possessed you, my daughter?" he whispered. "The lake is deep, nobody knows how deep, the two of you might have been drowned."

"How could we have drowned?" Comfort said sullen. Wasn't she wearing her red and yellow cloth for the power of life? Hadn't she rescued Jeo and brought him safely back? "I'm the best swimmer in my class, third in the whole junior school and I passed my Life Saving Certificate last term."

"Girls with life saving certificates, this is the English way," Mante said heavily. "But this is not England, Comfort. In Krempepong girls do not swim. The lake is sacred to the Ashanti people and girls and women are not allowed in it or on it. So it has always been. You have outraged the people of Krempepong after they received you kindly. In your English heart there is no respect for other people's ways."

"Sorry," Comfort said, the tears on her cheeks were hot now. "Sorry ... sorry ... I thought they would take Jeo away for ever ... take him to the Asantehene's palace ..."

"Aye-aye ... there is much you do not understand, Comfort," Mante said putting his arms round her. "Don't cry now, compose your thoughts. You are a grown woman to the people of Krempepong and the headman and the elders are waiting to see you."

"Stay with me," Comfort begged suddenly afraid, ashamed, grabbing at his hand as they walked away from the lake and towards the headman's house. "Please ..."

"Of course I will stay," Mante said. "You are my daughter and until you are married your fault is mine."

Pressure lamps hung at intervals along the veranda where the headman sat with his elders round him. His face was familiar, carpenter and boatbuilder for the village, he had greeted Comfort the evening before. But there was a strangeness about him now, arrayed as he was in the gold ornaments of his office, a hardness and unfamiliarity about all of them as they gazed fierce-eyed in Comfort's direction. She looked away, stared at the ground, her knees felt weak, she was frightened now. She had been frightened on the black lake but this was a different sort of fright.

"Comfort Kwatey-Jones you have outraged the custom," the headman said in Twi. "The lake is sacred to all the people of Krempepong, the lake is our father who feeds us and must be obeyed. No girl or women is allowed on the water. So it has always been."

"So it has always been," the elders muttered, nodding their heads.

"But my daughter is at boarding school in England," Mante broke in. "She does not speak much Twi, how can such a girl know the customs of Krempepong?"

"This is a serious crime and ignorance is no excuse," the headman went on steadily. "The lake, our father has been injured. He will not give us fish unless we appease him. Are we to starve because of this wild English girl?"

"No, no the girl must be drowned," the elders muttered. "The girl must be drowned in the lake."

"Long ago a girl was given to the lake every year."

"Comfort Kwatey-Jones must be given to the lake."

"Tell them I'm sorry," Comfort whispered catching the edge of her father's kente, not understanding the words but seeing their eyes and feeling their fury. Sorry in England, sorry in Wanwangeri, sorry in Krempepong Major too, was she going to be saying sorry all her life? "Perhaps ... if you tell him I'm half-Ga and half- English ... perhaps if you tell him I didn't know ..." Her voice trailed away under the fierce and disapproving gaze of the headman. "Sorry ... sorry... sorry."

"Does the girl understand the wrong she has done?" the headman asked.

"She understands now," Mante said. "She is contrite. Her ignorance is my fault, not hers, my neglect ... Perhaps the old man, the lake, will accept a libation ... a gift from me to remedy the crime? I have whisky in my car ..."

"A libation ... yes ... whisky ..." the elders muttered to each other.

"A libation is the modern way."

"The girl did not know the custom."

"Drowning was the old way."

"A libation must certainly be poured upon the lake shore and forgiveness begged," the headman said, his expression still severe. "And gifts must be offered too, to propitiate the injured spirit of the lake. What can you give, Comfort? What do you have of value? You must make some sacrifice."

"Sacrifice? Me? Well only this ..." Comfort said, looking from one to the other and not quite sure she had understood. She took the gold ring from around her neck, the ring Margaret had given to Mante long ago, the ring Mante had given to Comfort when she was eleven years old and which she had worn on a string round her neck ever since. "Does the old man ... does he like gold?"

"Perhaps ..." the headman said but the anger and resentment were still clear on his face. "Let us at least hope that gold and whisky will appease him."

Mante took her arm and they walked down to the shore of the lake and as they went the people came out of their huts and followed, keeping their distance. The moon was high and pale, covered with a thin veil of cloud, no longer making a glimmering road across the water. The flat dark surface of the lake was perfectly still, mysterious, as if deep in its heart the lake was brooding the injury done. On the far side there was a single light, a lamp held in a hand they couldn't see. Was it Peace standing there on the shore, Comfort wondered.

"Old man, our lake, our father accept this our offering," the headman intoned. He tipped the bottle pouring whisky onto the sand, three times north, three times south, three times east, three times west and at each tilt Comfort heard the whisky trickle onto the sand and its strong malty smell flavoured the night air. "Forgive this wild been-to girl who has broken your custom and travelled across your sacred surface. She must never return to Krempepong, she will never speak of her deed. Accept this pure gold ring, her sacrifice." The headman swung the ring back and forth on its string and then let go so it flew in an arc over the lake and landed with a faint splash. "Let there be plenty of fish."

"My ring, Margaret's ring," Comfort whispered biting her lip. Margaret had gone but her words and ways were alive inside Comfort for ever and she hardly needed a gold ring to hear them. And Mante stood beside her, powerful and strong in his kente. Mante who had spoken for her.

That night Comfort slept fitfully on the mat in Ya's hut. She could not forget the outrage of the chief's face, sounds of roistering mingled with her dreams of gold rings lost and silver fish sliding away down the silver streams and a girl drowning. In the morning she was awake and out early. The lake blue, pale as forget-me-nots, innocent in the daylight, dotted with fishing rafts. She stood in the trees just out of sight, watching and waiting. She might not be welcome near the lake.

It was Mante who came to the shore and cupped his hands and shouted boldly, "Is the catch good today, my friend?"

"Aye-aye . . . it is better today than yesterday," the

man on the nearest raft shouted back.

"We had better go while we can," Mante said softly as Comfort ran up to him. He put his arms round her shoulder and smiled down ruefully. "Before my daughter breaks another ancient custom. Go while the going is good, as they say in England."

"But I must go back to Wanwangeri," Comfort said. "I promised grandmother I'd be back by the full moon."

"So you shall," Mante said. "We will all go to Wanwangeri and my mother can see the new baby, Anan, and give him her blessing."

Chapter 15

An hour later they drove out of Krempepong Major in Mante's car. "Goodbye, goodbye and thank you for everything, thank you. We'll be back next month to pick up the car," Efua called gaily waving from the window. She sat in the front with Mante, the baby, Anan, asleep on her knees. Comfort and Jeo sat in the back with Mercy, another cousin of Efua's who would be the new nurse-girl. Comfort held Jeo on her lap. He seemed sad, disconsolate, his thumb in his mouth.

They drove along the track slowly. On either side the people of Krempepong lined their route, waving and smiling, calling their farewells, the outrage of the previous night apparently forgiven and forgotten in the bright light of day. Children leapt and grinned at the car windows, running alongside as the car bounced slowly along the rutted track.

Just before they reached the main road a girl darted from the bushes. "I come with you, I come back to Accra with Jeo ... please ... please ... me very good nurse-girl," Peace shouted running to keep pace with the car. "Please ..."

"What do you think?" Mante slowed the car.

"Let her come," Efua said. There was no mistaking Jeo's cry of joy, the brightness of his smile as he scrambled from Comfort's lap and snuggled against Peace. Comfort sighed and gazed out of the window at rows of cocoa trees with yellowing, almost ripe pods, her last look at Krempepong. The excitement and terror of the night before had gone and her whole body and limbs seemed invaded with a deep lassitude as if she could sleep for a hundred years. Did people in opium dens feel like this, Comfort wondered, had Sleeping Beauty.

For a moment the trees thinned as she saw the lake between them, blue as bird's eye, sparkling under the sun. A freshwater lake where villagers caught fish, a stretch of deep water that was all, and then the trees closed together again and the Krempepong lake and whatever it was or had been the night before was gone and Margaret's gold ring was gone and would lie in the lake forever now too; Comfort sighed, fingering Grandmother's amulet, all that was left round her neck to ease her sense of loss. 'Comfort Jones you have a long way to go.' But wherever Comfort went she could never come back to Krempepong.

She turned to look at the back of the heads in front of her, Mante's short-haired and Efua's wrapped in its matching headkerchief, both straight on their two strong necks, swinging a little as the car bumped but remaining upright like two ships' compasses. Her two parents, Comfort thought, it was not a thought she had ever had before but Efua was different since Anan was born, and Mante, her father, had saved her. What might have happened if he had not been there she did not dare think. At school his letters came so rarely that sometimes she wondered if he thought of her at all or found her simply an expensive nuisance. But Mante had been there and stood by her when she needed him. Suddenly Efua's head turned and her smile flashed, "Such a good baby, Anan," she whispered. "Sleeping again already." Her head dipped tenderly back to the child in her lap. Jeo resting against Peace closed his eyes.

Comfort was next to Mercy, who having never ridden in a car before, sat rigid and nervous beside her, eyes darting from side to side like frightened mice. Beyond her was Peace who kept silent, eyes lowered in penitence, her two arms clasped round Jeo and Lambkin. Suddenly Jeo opened his eyes, stared indignantly at Comfort for a moment and then closed them again. Comfort scuffled in the bundle at her feet. It was several days since she had written her diary.

August 28th, *Nearly got drowned in Krempepong lake*, she wrote. Now she was safe in the car she could think about the lake, how frightened she had been, water black as treacle below her and the rocking raft and the flower-frail moon above and Jeo screaming like ten murdered cats in her ear.

As well as fear there were questions too. If she hadn't fetched Jeo would he still be there in Krempepong Minor with Peace. Efua had agreed that he should stay there according to the chief. Would Mante have agreed too? What did she know of Mante? What did one really know of anybody? Everywhere the old ways were struggling with the new, the elders of Krempepong were the old ways, the elders of Krempepong who wanted her drowned. Six pairs of eyes watching her, beady and intent in the light of the pressure lamps, Comfort shivered so violently that Mercy turned towards her, startled. How would she ever forget the six pairs of eyes? *Nearly got drowned twice*, Comfort wrote. *Not going back to Krempepong Major ever. Anyway it's forbidden. Persona non grata.* Maybe Latin was some use after all.

She was travelling again, not just the journey to Wanwangeri and then to Accra and Heathrow and England, the journey through space, but travelling through time as well, leaving Krempepong Major and Wanwangeri still hardly touched by the twentieth century where life was much as it had been a hundred years before.

Already they were reaching the outskirts of Kumasi, made-up roads lined with trees, square white houses jostling with the ever increasing encroachment of shanty huts and wayside cooked-food stalls. Suddenly Jeo scrambled across Mercy and back onto Comfort's lap.

"Jeo," she whispered, folding her arms round him, feeling his warmth through her red and yellow cloth and a rush of joy which took her by surprise, filling her eyes with tears. Babies are the best thing in life, Margaret said and Jeo was still scarcely more than a baby.

But Jeo was her brother too, the reason why she had come to Krempepong, the reason why she had been excluded from Krempepong for ever and risked his life and her own. Jeo, heir to the chief of Krempepong, a little king, perhaps he would have been better if he had stayed in Krempepong Minor. She held him tight and kissed the springy top of his head. Perhaps he would have been better brought up in the old ways after all. What would he think when he grew up? What would he want? And what did she want, Comfort herself? She was back now wasn't she, inexorably set on the conveyor belt to Lodge School, French, Latin, netball, notices in the corridor, exams, brown and white bread on the tea table and huge bowls of red jam. And she had put herself back.

As the car moved slowly along the dusty track which ran between Akwapawa and Wanwangeri, Comfort stared out at the bushes and trees on either side. She knew every clump and branch, hadn't she lived here for almost six months two years ago, and not much in the natural world had changed since then. However slowly Mante drove because of the ruts, it was quicker than walking from Akwapawa after a day in the market. They passed two young men who stepped sideways from the track and looked after them. One raised his hand to wave and his face parted in a smile and then they rounded a bend and he was gone. Kwame, Comfort thought, her heart suddenly thudding so hard that surely Jeo must feel it against him and wake.

But Jeo slept on just as he had slept most of the journey and Peace leaning against Mercy, slept too. Only Mercy who had never been more than a day's walking distance from Krempepong before still stared about her wide-eyed.

"Is Wanwangeri, isn't it?" Efua said.

"Yes, Wanwangeri," Mante said hesitantly, frowning a little. He did not come often and new huts and compound fences had changed the outward profile of the village though customs might stay the same. Evidently they were expected. Grandmother, who often stayed in her hut for days at a time, stood at the compound entrance supported by her stick. Behind her were Ata and Esi and the children of the compound, all newly washed and smartly attired in the clothes normally reserved for school, bright-eyed and grinning shyly. Children came running from all round the village, jumping and pushing, alert to any possibility of excitement, something new to see.

"My son has come," Grandmother said in a quavery voice. "Praise be to Onyame, my son comes to visit his mother." She embraced Mante with tears running down her wrinkled cheeks but let him go almost immediately.

"Greetings, Efua, wife of Mante. Oh, let me see the new child, Anan. Oh, he is a fine-fine boy, look Esi ... Look Ata ... is he not just like his father?"

Comfort stood just behind, carrying the just woken Jeo and a moment later Grandmother turned towards them. "Jeo ... Little Jeo is come too. Aye-aye ... this child does not take after his father."

"He is like my family," Efua said and Jeo still half-asleep stopped in mid-yawn to say in Ga, a language he had not spoken for several weeks, "Greetings, my Grandmother, and good health and may Onyame be with you."

"Did you teach him that, Comfort?" Grandmother said delighted.

"It was Peace," Comfort said and Peace raised her eyes from the ground for a few seconds, her status enhanced by her well-mannered charge.

"His *adehye* blood speaks for itself," Peace murmured.

"Aye-aye ... the child talks sweetly and knows

what to say," Grandmother said dismissing this explanation and turning instead to Efua. "'The crab does not produce a bird', Mante was always honey-tongued, boy is more like his father than he looks."

There were further ceremonies to be performed, libations poured to the ancestors and thanks offered to the sky-family north, south, east, west, who had not only allowed the new child, Anan, to come but also allowed him to stay and be safely outdoored. The ceremonies done Grandmother sat on the stool in front of her hut with Anan on her knees and the others gathered round her. One gnarled finger gently stroked the sleeping baby's face. She seemed entirely absorbed with him, Comfort thought, and yet now and then she caught Grandmother's eyes resting upon her. Mante talked of his work and its demands, the numerous reasons why it was difficult for him to get to Wanwangeri. Explaining just why he couldn't come more often, seemed almost as much an obligation as coming. Nobody mentioned Krempepong or Efua's flight there in her red car, nor did they mention Comfort's journey across the lake, or her banishment from Krempepong. Did they know of it yet, Comfort wondered. Grandmother learned everything sooner or later from the talking drums.

"And where are my sisters' children?" Mante said, and since he had not been there for so long, the children of the compound who had been sitting in a big circle round them, were brought forward one by one in order of their age and introduced. Mante spoke to every child and gave his mother, Esi or Ata, fifty cedis for each child for school uniform and books. Evidently his observance of the custom had been agreed for, though Efua watched each transaction carefully, she continued to smile. That day in Wanwangeri it seemed everybody in the compound was smiling.

"Aye-aye ... my son understands what he must do at least," Grandmother said rocking on her stool. "'The fledging eagle soars to the sky but does not forget the nest'. Onyame be praised that I should live to see this day."

The sun was still rising and at the heat of the day the compound grew intolerable. After the midday meal Comfort took Peace and Jeo to her hut. Jeo settled at once on the new bed Tano had made for Comfort but Peace, not caring for beds, unwrapped the old sleeping mat and lay down.

Comfort lay on the opposite end of the bed to Jeo, already asleep. Last time she would lie in this bed, she thought. There were so many last times at Lodge School as the holidays approached. Last suppers and breakfasts, last cups of cocoa and more private last times, last time she would see Martin in the choir until next term, if his name was Martin. Her eyes moved round the hut and into the roof above. There were new wasp nests in the roof poles, little mud igloos, and more termite holes too. How long would it be before she slept there again and how many termite holes would there be by then?

She studied the sleeping Jeo over the scalloped edge of her own brown toes. His small face twitched. What was he dreaming, this small odd child, she wondered. The children of the compound were strictly disciplined and well-behaved and already Grandmother had looked askance at Jeo who helped himself to food before his turn. Half-Ga and half Ashanti, half-*adehye* and half-*omamba*, caught between the old ways and the new, did Jeo like herself belong nowhere after all? A flood of tenderness filled her throat and made her eyes hazy. All round them the compound was quiet. Everyone sleeping, children ejected from their huts on account of visitors lay in patches of shade where they could. But Comfort couldn't sleep. How was it she knew as well that Grandmother couldn't sleep either? Presently she swung her legs over the side of the bed and adjusted her cloth. As she stepped outside the sun beat down on her head like a hot griddle. Ata and her child lay sleeping in the narrow shade of the food store.

"Grandmother?" Comfort whispered into the doorway and the plastic ribbons quivered at her breath, the brilliant reds and blues already faded by the sun.

"Comfort."

She stepped inside and the ribbons fell back into place behind her with a faint hiss. Grandmother's mat lay unrolled to receive her but instead she was sitting on her stool, her chin resting on her stick and her eyes staring in front of her. A small smile flickered at her lips; was she thinking over the events of the morning or of long ago, or was she reading the talking drums, Comfort wondered, trying to listen but hearing no sound.

"Grandmother?" she said dropping onto the stool opposite.

"Aye-aye ... my Comfort," Grandmother said returning to the present. "So you have come back to me?"

"Tonight is the full moon," Comfort said. "And I said I would."

"You will always come back," Grandmother said. "However many moons that you stay away you will always come back because your heart is here in Wanwangeri. You cannot live without your heart."

The certainty in her voice, complacency almost, was irritating to Comfort, certain of nothing. But there was sadness, too, and resignation, because however certain Grandmother was of Comfort's return, that she would still be alive to see was far from certain. For a few moments the two of them sat side by side thinking these things and knowing the other thought them too.

"Stay here now," Grandmother begged suddenly. "You shall have a cocoa farm all your own. Joshua cannot repay the money borrowed, stay and let Joshua's farm be Comfort's, take Kwame for your husband if you want him."

Comfort blinked, catching a brilliant gleam in Grandmother's eyes deep in their wrinkled sockets, but something was pulling her the other way like a hundred silk threads. "I can't, Grandmother. A bit of my heart is in England too and I've got to go back to school."

"Chu, school," Grandmother snapped. "A grown woman, what has school to do with a grown woman? Will school bring you a cocoa farm of your own?" They stared at each other, locked together and divided by a particular mixture of love and something which was almost hate. "A young woman who has crossed the sacred Krempepong Lake, the only woman who has crossed the Krempepong lake and lived to talk of it."

"I do not talk of it," Comfort whispered head bowed. "And I never shall, I promised."

"You bring shame to us all."

"I'm sorry," Comfort said. "But I've got to go."

There was a long silence. Grandmother sighed and turned to rummage in a wooden chest at the back of the hut. "I have something for you," she said huskily and put it into Comfort's hand. It was small and made of wood.

"What is it?" Comfort said holding it up to the striped light from the doorway. "Oh, a lizard." It was intricately carved and weighed almost nothing. "Did Tano carve it?"

"This is not ... Tano's work ... it is very old," Grandmother said slowly with a long pause between each phrase. "It was given to me by my grandmother ... long ago ..." Now she stopped speaking and her head slid forward and she breathed the deep steady rhythm of sleep.

Comfort clutched the present in her hand. What could she give in return. She had nothing left to give ... except ... She slid out through the ribbons and ran back to her own hut. The presents she had bought had all been given long before. The Bob Geldof poster was the only precious thing she had. More blessed to give than to receive, hadn't the vicar taken that as his text on Sunday? She unhooked the poster carefully from the wall and carried it back.

"... a gift from my own grandmother," Grandmother said waking ten minutes later and resuming the conversation where she had left it. "And I am giving it to you."

"And I give this to you," Comfort said holding up the poster. "Bob Geldof who started Band Aid and Sport's Aid and who brought food and lorries to the starving people of Ethiopia ... and Africa ..."

"How did he do that?" Grandmother said staring

critically at the face through narrowed eyes. "Does he have a lorry-business like me? Is he a rich man or a big person in the government?"

"Well no ... well ... he's just magic," Comfort said gazing at the poster, bereft. Her fingers longed to grab it back. How would she manage without it? She could get another poster of course but it wouldn't be the one she had taken all round Ghana with her. Saying goodbye to Bob Geldof was like parting with a brilliant friend ... worse.

"Magic?" Grandmother stared at the poster. "Is he a priest then?"

"Not exactly ..." Comfort said.

"Aye-aye ... put him on the wall opposite the postcards."

"Every month I will send you another postcard," Comfort said impaling the poster on small nails in the wall. Her eyes prickled with tears. "Two postcards every month, I promise." Old churches of the Romney Marshes, sepia kittens with crimson bows, views of Folkstone, what sort of postcards would Bob Geldof like?

Around them the compound was waking, cooking had started for the evening meal. There was eating to be done and talking, news and greetings to be exchanged with the people of Wanwangeri, the baby admired and final farewells to be said. By the time it was all accomplished it was already dark.

"Goodbye, my mother," Mante said embracing her briefly and getting straight into the car. Efua and Anan were already in the front, Peace, Mercy and Jeo in the back.

"Onyame be with you, my son," Grandmother said.

"Goodbye, Grandmother," Comfort said, but Grandmother had gripped her arm tightly.

"Stay for another day?" she whispered and turned to the car. "Let Comfort stay for another day or two. It is four days to the plane. She can catch the lorry down to Accra. She is used to travelling. Or I will send *Dry Leaf Fall* down with her."

"Yes … but …" Comfort murmured, wanting to go, wanting to stay too, Grandmother's grip like a tourniquet on her arm. If she didn't go now by car she knew she would never go, there would be delays and obstructions until after a bit she wouldn't want to go, couldn't. She realised Grandmother knew this too.

"Just for two days?" Mante said looking from one to the other doubtfully. He found it hard to deny his mother anything. "Well … but …" In Peace's arms in the back of the car, Jeo began to cry noisily. A flicker of annoyance passed across Mante's face. "I think Comfort had better come with us. I myself have had so little time with her … too little time."

"Goodbye, Grandmother," Comfort slipped quickly into the back of the car and the screaming stopped as Jeo subsided onto her lap and hiccupped into silence. As the car drove out of the village, Comfort looked back waving from the back window. Several figures were standing there, dark under the round moon. Ata and Esi and Tawia and Kwame, large and strong and unsmiling, his arms raised in a final salute. Grandmother had already disappeared.

The car slid through Akwapawa and took the main road south. Dark grey forest under the moon. She had been back at Wanwangeri for the full moon as she had promised, Comfort thought idly, and she had left it by the full moon too. When would she return? Jeo slept in her arms. She took Grandmother's present out of the waist of her cloth and held it forward so Efua and Mante could see it in the dashboard light. "Look, a lizard, it's very old."

"A chameleon," Mante corrected her and she saw his lips twitch to a small smile. "Yes, a chameleon. The chameleon changes colour according to its background, that is how it survives."

Chapter 16

The table was out on the veranda at 3, Hillside Estate, laid ready for the evening meal. Did you always have to eat two dinners travelling, Comfort wondered. The ornate silver cutlery gleamed silver in the lamplight and the sitting room parquet was perilous where John had celebrated the homecoming with an outbreak of polishing. Comfort looked down at the green-striped plate and thought of the broken cup and Efua's last breakfast before she ran off. She looked covertly at Efua and wondered if she was thinking of it too.

"Very good Missus go come home, very good pikkin go come home," John said putting the dishes of rice and curried chicken on the table with a wide smile and distinct sense of occasion. Was it one of the Backyard-Farm-in the City chickens, Comfort wondered, but did not want to ask, not wanting to know. Actually she felt quite hungry.

"New pikkin fine-fine boy, Missus."

"Thank you, John, it's good to be home again," Efua said, her tranquil smile confirmed the sea-change that had come with Anan's birth. "Home for Comfort, only for a few days, soon she will fly away home to England like the ladybird," Efua sighed gustily. "We shall miss you, Comfort."

"Will you?" Comfort mumbled, pushing out her lower lip and wondering. She tried to be pleased at the new accord, the new friendliness between Efua and Mante but now and then on the journey she had seen a smile passing between them that had nothing to do with her, that excluded her, and she didn't like it. "Well I haven't gone yet, have I?" Could she still stay if she wanted, if they wanted? Suppose Mante suddenly asked her, begged her, got her a place at Achimota School or Aburi Girls say, to be a weekly boarder and see Jeo every weekend, little Jeo, and Grandmother every holidays. She turned her head and stared into the darkness round them imagining how it would be. The veranda made a square island of light. The bungalow next door was checked with windows, amber coloured in the warm darkness, she could hear voices, laughter. Perhaps she would get to know the Americans next door after all. She would miss Lodge School of course, Maxine and Suzanne and Granny and Grandad at Penfold … Lettie. But how much would she miss them?

"Four more days," her father glanced at his watch. "What time is your plane, Comfort?" Did he want her to go?

"Aye-aye … there has been so little time to talk," Efua said. "Comfort has not even told me what the fashion colours are now, the latest thing … Here it is nothing but old-fangled fashion … black-market fashions at Shylock prices. Aye-aye … our chameleon been-to daughter will soon fly away …"

She turned her head at the slap of Mercy's sandals on the veranda.

"Scuse please, Missus, baby him cry-cry."

"Aye-aye … your son is hungry. Your son is all the time hungry … just like his father," Efua said getting up from the table with her plate of curry in her hand but her smile was teasing.

"Like father, like son?" Mante's laugh rumbled in his chest. "'A crab does not produce a bird'."

"What old-fangled talk is this?" Efua said swaying her hips so her cloth swung out as she walked away.

"It was so different with Jeo," Mante said leaning back in his chair and smiling still. He seemed to be speaking almost to himself. "Such crying, such nights … the bottle fed child is restless they say … Efua went back to work soon after he was born … Jeo is restless still. Such crying … such crying."

"Perhaps it's the *adehye* blood, perhaps he's more sensitive," Comfort said. "Perhaps I should have left him?"

"How left him?" Her father had turned towards her sharply, his eyebrows had reached almost to his hair.

"Left him in Krempepong Minor," Comfort said. "He didn't cry there, he didn't cry at all there. Perhaps he would be better off in Krempepong Minor. If I'd left him on the other side of the lake would you have fetched him?"

"Of course," Mante said conceding, "maybe I should have left him for a month or two … left him for the cocoa harvest … a child should know all his family … all the festivals. Jeo belongs to different worlds … he must know them both … the old and the new. Peace takes good care of him. It is good that Jeo learns African ways … the old ways … the things I never learned or soon forgot. He will be chief one day. His uncle is the next chief, surgeon at the big new hospital here. Will he neglect his patients for his village? Or is it the people of Krempepong Minor who will be neglected?" He cut himself a second slice of pineapple, pulling the slice in half and munching at the fibrous yellow flesh.

"And you think that's wrong?" Comfort said.

"Right or wrong who can say?" Mante shrugged. "Old and new, black and white, peasant economy or western technology ... we must all learn to live in several worlds." He tossed the pineapple core over the veranda wall. "Sometimes these worlds are irreconcilable, Comfort, my daughter. This waste of double aims ... of seeking to reconcile what cannot be reconciled ... ends in frustration ... exhaustion."

"Our chameleon daughter, what did Efua mean?" Comfort said staring into the darkness. What had Grandmother meant by the gift, that Comfort was infirm of purpose, changeable like the chameleon? "Ansi Grandmother?"

"Who understands your grandmother?" Mante said softly. "The chameleon is clever, changing to match its background, it is always safe. Aye-aye ... we must all be chameleons nowadays."

"Not you," Comfort said. "You match all right where you are."

"How can my daughter say such things?" Mante said. "I do not talk only of skin. The background here is changing fast and such changes are painful, very painful indeed. Ghana is an independent country, yes, but now we must kneel to new masters, Integrated Marketing Programme and House Cleaning and Devaluation when prices double overnight and we have new Gods too, World Bank and International Monetary Fund, instead of the entrails of a goat we examine these new oracles. Aye-aye ... we all have to change to fit in the modern world. Once we struggled to be book-clever, Latin-clever, but now we must be computer-clever ... but best of all is change-clever ... adaptable. Be change-clever, Comfort, like a chameleon."

"But some one like me ... I can't change my colour, can I?" Comfort said. "And I don't belong anywhere ... not anywhere at all?" Comfort said trying to laugh but it sounded more like a sob. "Talk about crazy-mixed-up kid."

"Chu, what is this old-fangled nonsense my daughter is talking?" Mante said. "Mixed blood is the future, isn't it? Mixed blood is great, creative conflict, the best of both worlds. Everything comes from somewhere else, Comfort, even our famous 'dash.' It came with the Portuguese in the sixteenth century, 'Dache'. James Bannerman, Lieutenant Governor of the Gold Coast, African mother, European father, Bob Marley, Casely Hayford, Jerry Rawlings himself. Mixture makes something new, new ideas, this is what we need. In the old world it was wars and fighting for territory but in the new world this cannot be or none of us will survive. We need new ideas, new ways of doing things, of sorting out conflict. Flexibility, that is the best gift of the fairy godmother; be a survivor, my Comfort, a chameleon."

"My heart will not change," Comfort said flatly.

"Of course not, the Ghanaian heart is truly formidable, the great Ghanaian heart and you have a bit of it, Comfort, your heart will always be here."

Last night in Ghana, Comfort wrote for September 2nd, sitting on her bed and looking out through mosquito netting like brown chiffon. She could see the waning moon through it but not the stars. Around her the house was perfectly quiet, Efua sleeping, Mante in his study. Far away a drum was beating. One day she would read the talking drums. *I am a chameleon,* she wrote. A chameleon could fit in anywhere. Everywhere.

Her case perched on top of the chest of drawers, everything ready packed except for her night things and her green school blazer and jeans hanging on the chair ready for the journey, jeans and blazer was a compromise, a chameleon had to compromise.

On the other side of the room Jeo slept in his white cot shining pearl-like in the moonlight. Peace who had always slept in the camp bed beside him, had fitted her camp bed between the legs of the cot. Little Jeo would need to be a chameleon too, Comfort thought, if he had to go to school and live at Hillside half the time and live in Krempepong and learn to be a chief as well.

I shall miss Ghana and Jeo and Efua and Mante and Anan, she wrote, *and Grandmother and Ata and Tawia and everybody.* Some things would be lost forever, Joshua's farm for instance, who would get that. Comfort sighed and slid her diary into her blazer pocket.

"Might as well take us to the front gate while you're about it," Granny said. "Right to our own front door, that's service, that is," she added with a little laugh which contrived to be both embarrassed at the luxury and pleased at getting her money's worth.

"Right you are," Frank Jarrett said nosing the taxi forward. The lane was almost submerged under burgeoning summer hedges and the long flattened grass of the village green.

"All this travelling wears me out," Granny said, starting up the path while Grandad paid for the taxi. "And now there's the supper to get."

"Shall I get it?" Comfort said lugging her heavy case over the doorstep and depositing it on the sitting room floor. "I easily could."

"No, no, dear, it's all ready. I left it all ready this morning. Heating up the soup doesn't take me a minute. You're not getting *croutons*, mind, I don't feel up to *croutons* at my time of life, not after all this travelling. And don't leave your case there for Grandad to trip over, whatever next?"

Comfort started up the stairs, up and round, up and round. "Mind the wall," Granny called after her. "I washed your netball kit ready." In the middle of the attic bedroom she touched the ceiling with her hands. She could tell she was taller. She took the chameleon out of her pocket and put it on the dressing table. Home was where your chameleon was, from now on.

The sky was pigeon grey and the chestnut tree along the side of the church already had yellow at the edge of its lower leaves. Lettie would be home by now, doing her homework in her bedroom or not doing her homework in her bedroom.

Below the window a bell tinkled in the front garden, the cowbell Granny had brought back from Switzerland.

"Supper's all ready," Granny added for good measure.

"Know that poinsettia I gave you," Comfort said

sitting down. "Well they've got them in Ghana growing wild, Ashanti blood they call them."

"Real bobby dazzler that poinsettia. Little fellow still got that woolly lamb you made for him?" Grandad said spooning up soup.

"He takes it everywhere," Comfort said. For an instant Krempepong lake flashed in her head like switching on the telly, Jeo clinging to her neck and screaming. There was a tremor in her voice as she added, "He likes it a lot."

"Funny that," Granny observed. "A child like that, in Africa."

"Jeo and me have the same spirit," Comfort said. "Because a child's spirit comes from the father."

"That's one way of looking at it," Granny said.

"And your grandmother, how's she keeping? Must be a good age?"

"She's okay," Comfort said. "She says her grandmother was Ashanti. She wanted me to stay as a matter of fact."

"My grandmother was Irish," Grandad said hurriedly.

"Stay?" Granny put down her spoon and picked up a morsel of bread. "How could you possibly stay? What about your exams, your mocks coming up next term? Did you tell her you were second in the form?"

"Not exactly," Comfort said. "Well it didn't come up ... anyway she wanted me to leave school. I mean she was going to give me a cocoa farm if I stayed. She gave me a small farm of my own last time but well this was Joshua's cocoa farm and he borrowed money from Grandmother a year ago and he can't pay it back, so he has to give her his farm, I mean it was a proper big farm like you get in England ..." Comfort finished.

209

"Goodness gracious me," Granny said, her eyes very blue over the tomato soup. "Whatever good would a farm be to you?"

"Poor Joshua," Grandad said. "Losing his farm like that."

"Well ... because I'm her granddaughter ... and she wanted me to stay," Comfort said.

"Cupboard love," Granny said very precisely. "I'm your grandmother too and it's nice to have you back. But don't go expecting any cocoa farms or anything else, young lady. You've got to pass your exams and stand on your own two feet."

"I know," Comfort said. There was a pause while Grandad gathered the soup plates together and put them through the hatch.

"Course there's degrees and things in agriculture nowadays," Granny said. "Lucky you've got the brains, Comfort, well your father was clever, no doubt about that. There's plenty of girls do agriculture nowadays ... and then there's economics ... what did you get for maths? We ought to have a look at 'Which University?', they've got it in the library."

"That's going on a bit isn't it?" Grandad said. "Our Comfort's only fourteen. It is fourteen, isn't it, Comfort?"

"Fourteen's grown-up in some places," Comfort said. "My cousin, Ama, got married at fourteen and she's got a baby now."

"Humph," Granny said. "Well you've got other things to think about I'm glad to say. Ham or tongue? I got a nice bit of tongue from the shop especially.

"Ham, please," Comfort said.

"Did you finish your book, 'Tess of the d'Urbevilles'?"

"Not quite," said Comfort crossing her fingers.

"Did you tell Frank Jarrett to be here at ten o'clock sharp?" Granny said. "All this travelling wears me out, Heathrow today, Folkestone tomorrow ..."

"Oh, can't I go on my own?" Comfort said. "Honestly, I'll be quite all right."

"She's been half across the world on her own, what's Folkestone to a seasoned traveller?" Grandad winked the eye furthest from Granny.

"That's as maybe. She's not going back to school on her own," Granny said. "Suppose something was to happen ... the things you see in the papers ... I couldn't look myself in the face if I'd let her go on her own, I'd never forgive myself ... never."

"I think I'll go to bed," Comfort said.

Ten minutes later she got into bed and then leaned up on one elbow. Her head was throbbing oddly and nothing she looked at kept quite still. September 2nd, *Back at Smithy Cottage*, she wrote. *Granny and Grandad fetched me from Heathrow.* Her eyes circled the small cream-walled attic, traces of blue-tac where Bob Geldof had been. Perhaps she would hang her cloth there, red and yellow for the power of life.

The window looked black with the light on and outside an owl hooted. There was an owl in the churchyard, Lettie said. Beneath the floorboards the bed creaked as Granny sat down. "Been a long day," she muttered. "Thank God for bed."

Everything just the same, Comfort wrote. But it wasn't just the same, nothing stayed quite the same, not really. *Granny just the same anyway*. It was no good trying to change people, Margaret said. Why should you want to change people, Comfort wondered. Granny would go on saying the things she said and being the way she was as long as she breathed. And as long as she breathed she would go on doing her best for Comfort too. Nothing Comfort did or said would change that. And that was all right, Comfort thought, that was safe. As they said in Wanwangeri, 'When you cross the river never insult the alligator until you have passed him'. So many rivers to cross. 'Comfort Jones you have a long way to go'.

Nobody had told her about her white great grandparents before. *I am one-sixteenth Ashanti and seven-sixteenths Ga and two-sixteenths Irish and two sixteenths Scottish and one-sixteenth Welsh and three sixteenths English*, Comfort wrote. She was a mixture all right. "'Mix is great'," Mante said. *Back to school tomorrow. Maybe I'll write to Ruby.* Joleen would know Ruby's address most likely. She could do what she wanted.

She was tired, perhaps it was jet lag that nothing would keep still. On the cream wall opposite where Bob Geldof had been, images jigged and flickered like an amateur film and went on even when she closed her eyes, projecting against her inner eyelids. Dream-seeing some people called it, she was looking at Hillside, Winnie was back in quarters, she could see and almost hear them laughing, Winnie and Mercy and Peace, Jeo holding Lambkin and watching them with wide cornelian eyes. Then Wanwangeri where Grandmother leaned her head on her stick and listened to Joshua pleading, couldn't he stay just one more year, she nodded her consent. Akwapawa market and the lake at Krempepong where Margaret's gold ring would lie for ever, moved slowly and flickering across the wall, all the people she knew, her family, all the places she had been. And after, more shadowy still, elusive as thought, people she didn't know and places she had never seen, a line of African children dancing and waving, nine little children. "Who are you?" Comfort said waking herself from dream-seeing and knowing that same instant who they were. The might-have-been-places, the might-have-been-babies who would never be born now, hers and Kwame's.

Comfort blinked and closed her eyes but the pictures didn't come back. *Kwame gone*, she wrote and closed the diary.

"See you in two years, Comfort, my daughter," Mante had said. She would be sixteen then and Jeo would be nearly five. She would go to Wanwangeri of course but Kwame would have married long before, dancing and drumming under the moon, other children born.

Below her the bed creaked louder as Granny got into it. "It's no good," she said and her voice rose slightly. "I'll never understand you, Barty, If I live to a hundred. Wanting to let my own granddaughter travel all that way to Folkstone by herself ... with all the things you see in the papers ... a girl of fourteen, a girl like Comfort."

Comfort switched out the light. An almost full moon sailed in the dark Kentish sky, were they drumming and dancing under the same moon in Wanwangeri, she wondered. "I am a chameleon," Comfort whispered and closed her eyes.